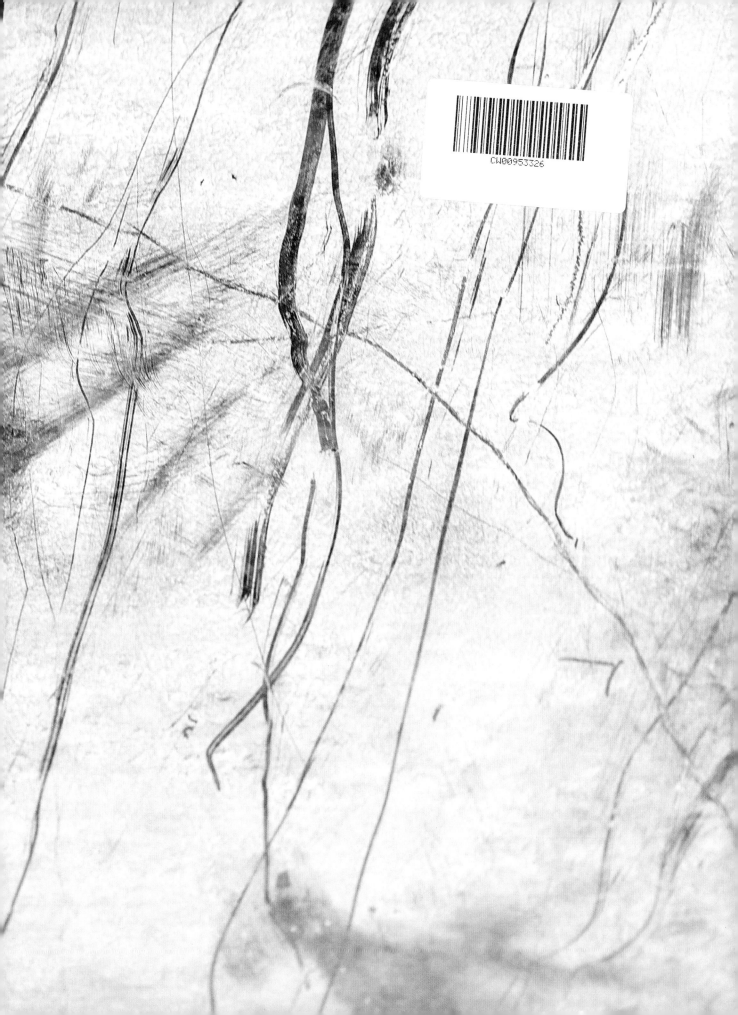

PARADISE AND PLENTY
A ROTHSCHILD
FAMILY GARDEN

PARADISE AND PLENTY

A ROTHSCHILD FAMILY GARDEN

MARY KEEN

PHOTOGRAPHY BY TOM HATTON

PIMPERNEL
PRESS LTD
www.pimpernelpress.com

Pimpernel Press Limited
www.pimpernelpress.com

Paradise and Plenty
A Rothschild Family Garden
Copyright © Pimpernel Press Limited 2015
Text copyright © Mary Keen 2015

Photographs copyright
© The Waddesdon Estate 2015
except for the reproduction of
The Greenhouse: Cyclamen and Tomatoes
by Eric Ravilious on pages 112–113
copyright © Tate, London 2015

First Pimpernel Press edition 2015

Designed by Dean Pauley

A catalogue record for this book is available from
the British Library.

ISBN 978-1-9102-5812-5

Typeset in Arnhem
Printed and bound in China

9 8 7 6 5 4 3 2 1

Title page
In the topiary garden, a shepherd devised by
the eighteenth-century sculptor John Cheere is
surrounded by clipped shapes in box, yew and
Lonicera nitida.

CONTENTS

FOREWORD

This splendid book documents an extensive walled garden deep in the English countryside, where the emphasis is on virtuoso horticulture. It is a perfect dream of a place, managed by one of the most brilliant gardeners of our era. If you are a home gardener looking for inspiration, you will find it here. If you are a garden historian searching out old traditions, read on. If you are a professional hoping to learn new tricks, you have come to the right place. Or if you are an armchair gardener looking to escape to a magical realm behind high walls, where no one but you will be invited, this book is for you.

The garden is a feature of the estate called Eythrope, a private domain adjacent to the Rothschild family's grand Victorian chateau at Waddesdon. The walls and the courtyard complex of buildings within were built in the late nineteenth century by the passionate gardener Alice Rothschild, who lived next door at Waddesdon and created Eythrope as a retreat from the formal splendour of the main house.

In our day, three fascinating personalities have collaborated to reinvent the garden at Eythrope. They are Lord Rothschild, whose garden it is today and who cares deeply about it. And Mary Keen, the celebrated gardener and writer, who, at Lord Rothschild's request, designed the garden that now occupies the enclosed site. And Sue Dickinson, the gifted head gardener, who, with her team, grows superlative vegetables, fruits, glasshouse tomatoes, auriculas, cutting flowers and many other vibrantly healthy plants, all arranged in the most artistic fashion and topped off by a thrilling pair of herbaceous borders running down the middle just for pleasure. The garden has been restored to its original function – to supply produce and flowers for the family of the owner. But it is a work of art as well.

As works of art and private places, enclosed gardens are always intriguing. The walls were usually built for practical reasons and protection, of course – from cold, wind, wildlife, and the neighbours. But, practicality aside, our imaginations are stirred by visions of gardens such as the Potager du Roi at Versailles, the Mexican courtyard garden of Frida Kahlo, George Washington's kitchen garden at Mount Vernon, or the circular Botanical Garden of Padua, where the walls were erected in 1552 to keep nearby residents from stealing medicinal plants.

One summer day two years ago, I had the enormous pleasure of visiting the garden at Eythrope with Mary Keen. Of course my friends among the horticultural cognoscenti had told me about this remarkable place, and I knew of Lord Rothschild's devotion to it and his interest in doing everything right. I had heard about the much-admired Sue Dickinson, who had achieved the miraculous. And I knew that Mary Keen had introduced these worthy partners to one another.

But I was certainly not prepared for the incredibly high standard of the gardening. It is quite flawless, as the photographs in the book illustrate. In the course of the visit I began to see, and now that I have

Opposite
A bust of *America*,
brought from the Aviary
at Waddesdon Manor,
presides over a corner of
the glasshouse.

read the text of this book I have learned, that this level of excellence is achieved by the refinement of traditional methods, the introduction of new and scientific improvements, and great skill on the part of the gardeners, all of which is combined with marvellous taste, insistence on perfection, total focus on results, and hard work.

My favorite example of Sue Dickinson's high-end horticultural practice is described in the 'Fruit' section of this book – it is the growing of cherries. On my desk here in New York I have a snapshot I took that day as Sue and Mary walked me around. It is an image of a rabbit's tail affixed to a long stick. These elegant cherries (of several old varieties) are grown in handsome terracotta pots. Sue explained to me that every day at noon, during the flowering season of the cherries, they are pollinated with the furry tail-on-a-stick, just as they have been for generations in this historic garden. Perhaps before you even begin to read this book you will delight yourself by turning to page 81 to learn about the cultivation of the cherries. No task in your own garden will ever again seem too detailed.

The trio of personalities who have created the garden have now collaborated again to make this book and share the garden's beauty, and the technologies that make it awesome, with us and with future gardeners who will most certainly not be exposed to such a gardening tradition. We are all in the debt of the makers – for the place and for the book.

Gregory Long
President
The New York Botanical Garden
August 2014

INTRODUCTION

There are plenty of books about gardens, but this one is different. The walled kitchen garden at Eythrope does something remarkable, on a scale that is unique. Fruit, vegetables and flowers are grown for a country house where entertaining still happens on a grand scale and where everything has always been done to the highest possible standards.

The garden at Eythrope forms part of the Waddesdon estate and its history belongs to the history of the family who made the place famous. The garden was laid out in its present form a quarter of a century ago, when the present Lord Rothschild inherited the running of Waddesdon and moved into the Pavilion at Eythrope, which has always been the dower house for the Manor at Waddesdon. Sue Dickinson, who trained at Waterperry, the legendary training college for women gardeners, has been in charge of the garden from the start. Under her inspired management, the place has been a focus for excellence among gardening cognoscenti.

Most English country houses have reluctantly abandoned their large and intensive gardens because of the expense of maintenance. In the early years of the last century, all large houses were proud of being self-sufficient. After the two world wars, many kitchen gardens were grassed over, or reduced to a half or a quarter of their original size. They were turned into orchards, or places for pigs or poultry, with a small patch for vegetables and a few bushes of soft fruit. The concept of growing fruit under glass almost ceased to exist, and the range of flowers grown for cutting for the house was drastically reduced.

Even at Eythrope, before Lord Rothschild inherited, the kitchen garden had been adapted for semi-commercial purposes. Many of the greenhouses were fragile, and the garden was barely a going concern. Now, with a restored layout and with everything in running order, almost nothing is bought for the house, all year round. Everything at Eythrope is home-grown, and grown to perfection. There are whole greenhouses dedicated to the growing of tomatoes, or scented-leaf pelargoniums. Figs, grapes, apricots, peaches and cherries are grown under glass. Outside, even in the worst and wettest summer of 2012, while other gardeners were lamenting the lack of crops, at Eythrope the vegetables, fruit and flowers were still being harvested in a state of near perfection.

This may not seem relevant to the average gardener, who will never run a place on a similar scale, but the attention to detail at all stages of production is something anyone might copy. As more and more people turn to growing their own, information is needed about the techniques of dedicated cultivation, as well as the results. Many of the techniques used at Eythrope are old and tried, but are now hardly known beyond its walls. Meticulous garden records are kept by each of the six gardeners who work in the walled garden. From these diaries and from talking to the men and women who produce the crops there is a lot to be learned.

It is a modern tendency to want instant results, but a successful garden is not a product that can be effortlessly manufactured from the pages of a glossy magazine. Gardening is a process that takes time. Just as Olympic athletes must undergo hours of unseen and often dull and demanding training before they can win a gold medal, a garden needs dedication in all weathers to reach perfection. The Eythrope team work through dark days and on ones when it is too hot for most of us to venture outside. What they do is meticulously organized and executed.

Eythrope has been open very occasionally for charity, but otherwise it has always been kept intensely private. The idea of a book to celebrate its outstanding and consistent achievement came about because it seemed sad not to share the secrets and delights of this remarkable garden with other gardeners. And as an exercise in the conservation of old methods and traditional techniques it cannot, even with a Rothschild purse, be continued in the same way and on the same scale for ever. Few of us could hope to emulate Eythrope, or the efforts of the gardeners, but even if most readers can take home only 50 per cent of the advice that this book contains, they will have better gardens and a better understanding of how the highest standards can be achieved.

The book is arranged thematically. The chapter openers are general descriptions of what happens in each area and each of these is followed by three or four garden operations which are illustrated and described in more detail. The background work, the *how* that is needed to deliver the produce, is shown in black and white, but the finished results – the *wow* pictures that appear in each chapter – are in colour. I hope the descriptions of the work that accompany the build-up photographs are clear. I certainly learned a lot about how things should be done as I wrote the book over the course of two gardening years.

The appendices contain even more detailed information than the seven growing chapters, with lists of plants grown, and notes on seed collection and the timing of seed sowing. Included, too, are short biographies of each member of the gardening team, because without their dedicated work the garden would not exist.

Paradise and Plenty is intended to be a record of the way things have been done at this unique place for almost a quarter of a century under the present management, and a way of sharing the knowledge that has been passed down from Miss Alice's gardeners to the modern team. It is also a tribute to Lord Rothschild, the present owner, to his forebear Miss Alice, and to Sue Dickinson (described by Robin Lane Fox as 'the number one seed among professional gardeners'), who conserves not only a wonderful Victorian garden but also gardening methods that were developed over many preceding centuries. And it is dedicated to all working gardeners who grow things to the highest possible standards.

Mary Keen
November 2014

Waddesdon 1885.

THE ROTHSCHILDS AT
WADDESDON AND EYTHROPE

The English branch of the global empire that was the Rothschild business was well established by the end of the nineteenth century. By that time, several members of the close-knit family had settled near one another, in the beautiful Vale of Aylesbury, in Buckinghamshire.

Becoming a landowner has always been the route to social advancement in England. A century earlier, another banker, Henry Hoare, bought Stourhead to anchor the Hoare dynasty to Wiltshire. In Georgian England, bankers were lower in the social scale than they are today. Henry Hoare's father was a horse-dealer; his son and grandson were anxious to distance themselves from their origins and to prove that they were civilized gentlemen who read Virgil and travelled on the Grand Tour. The early nineteenth-century Rothschilds, being Jewish and in trade, were far from accepted by the established aristocracy. Like Henry Hoare, the Rothschilds wanted to tie their provenance to the past. Their route to security was through buying the possessions of emperors and kings. They built houses like chateaux, took up hunting and cultivated their gardens, but above all they collected beautiful things and entertained lavishly, living in a style that became known as '*le goût* Rothschild'. Determined to stick together, they bought thousands of acres of southern England when the agricultural depression saw many landed estates come on to the market. On a clear day, the cousins might have waved to one another from the roofs of Tring, Waddesdon, Mentmore, Ascott, Aston Clinton and Halton.

By far the most important of these houses was Waddesdon, the only one that today survives intact with all its collections. Baron Ferdinand de Rothschild bought the estate from the Duke of Marlborough in 1874. Tragically, the Baron's marriage to his cousin Evelina in 1865 had lasted for only eighteen months before she died in childbirth. He never married again. But after eight years in mourning he was finally able to put aside his sorrow, and at Waddesdon he built himself a fairytale palace in the style of a French Renaissance chateau. Here he planned to house his growing collections and entertain a small circle of friends. The French architect Gabriel-Hippolyte Destailleur was engaged to design a house on top of one of the few hills in the Aylesbury Vale. It was surrounded by gardens laid out by Elie Lainé. Statues, fountains and an aviary were conjured from nowhere and fully grown trees were dragged to the site, on carts drawn by teams of sixteen Percheron horses imported from France. Later, with hindsight, the Baron wrote, 'But if I may venture to profit a word of advice to anyone who may feel inclined to follow my example – it is to abstain from planting old trees, limes and chestnuts perhaps excepted.' It still makes sense to plant young trees rather

Opposite
Cecile Hofer,
Waddesdon Manor, 1885.

17

than expensive mature specimens. Baron Ferdinand's lavish garden-making did not stop at trees. It was said at the time that the number of bedding plants used by a landowner was a good indication of their status. A squire might have 10,000 plants, a baronet 20,000, an earl 30,000 and a duke 40,000, but the Baron's huge parterre went one better. At Waddesdon, 41,000 plants were planted overnight, with four bedding changes a year.

At the centre of this fabulous place was a young man of thirty-five, alone but for the company of his younger sister, Alice. After Ferdinand's wife died, Alice had left the Rothschild house outside Frankfurt to be with him in England, where they both became English subjects. Once Waddesdon was built, brother and sister were to live together at the vast house for over twenty years.

The Baron was a perfectionist, which is, as a later Rothschild pointed out, a costly habit. But when he died aged fifty-nine, his obituary described a man for whom 'beneficence had been the business of his life.' These two qualities, perfectionism and generosity, were characteristic of many generations of Rothschilds, and Ferdinand's spinster sister, always known as 'Miss Alice', who became the owner of Waddesdon after his death, was no exception. Lady Battersea (herself born a Rothschild) wrote of Miss Alice, 'At Waddesdon her rule was a very determined if a generous one . . . managing her property, looking after every detail of her estate undeterred by any opposition she might meet with.' Her housekeeping standards – 'Miss Alice's rules' – are still judged conservation best practice. She instigated blinds and covers to limit light exposure and would allow no one to handle objects in the collection except in silence and wearing white gloves. She was also passionately interested in the garden. The colourful three-dimensional bedding which can still be seen at Waddesdon today was started by Miss Alice. And in her day the gardeners referred to the kitchen garden – an area devoted entirely to the production of fruit, vegetables and flowers which were grown to furnish the Manor – as Paradise.

Building appears to be in the Rothschild genes. While her brother was supervising works at the Manor, Miss Alice occupied herself with the neighbouring property at Eythrope. Here in 1875 she began to create the Pavilion, her Trianon, where she might retreat from the splendours of her brother's establishment. The site of Lord Chesterfield's old house, which was demolished in 1810, had been near the river, but Miss Alice was frail and suffered from rheumatic fever, so she instructed George Devey (a favourite architect of both old and new money at the time) to design a small house higher up on the site. Devey's usual style was Olde Englishe, but the Pavilion he made for Miss Alice was in the Jacobean style, with two turrets and Frenchified windows, like those at her brother's house, but on a miniature scale. The house had no bedrooms. Eythrope was considered too damp for Miss Alice to sleep there, so every night she was driven the three miles back to Waddesdon. The Pavilion was designed to be a modest place where she could spend the day and,

Frederick Tayler, *Miss Alice de Rothschild Hunting*, late nineteenth century.

The planting of the Waddesdon parterre, *c.* 1910.

One of Miss Alice's giant wirework birds, at the entrance to Waddesdon, *c.* 1910.

above all, a place for her to make her own garden. Later her great-niece, the distinguished scientist Miriam Rothschild, would say that, for Miss Alice, her gardens replaced the children she never had.

By 1890 a park and a garden of sixty acres had been created at Eythrope from what the *Journal of Horticulture* described as 'formerly little more than a swamp and a wilderness'. There were twenty acres of 'soft fresh green turf in excellent keeping'. There were shrubberies, clumps of rhododendrons, specimen trees and flower beds. Miss Alice had a rose garden, a Dutch garden, a Mexican garden, a grotto near an enlarged lake, as well as both a wilderness and a wild garden. The Pavilion was embowered in climbing plants – roses, clematis, Virginia creepers and ivies. There was a tiny parterre in imitation of the one at Waddesdon; and there was a four-acre walled kitchen garden, with three huge glasshouses for flowering plants and five smaller working greenhouses for propagation. 'Eythrope', Edward Hamilton, Gladstone's secretary, wrote in 1898, 'is the most magnificent horticultural toy seen anywhere. She [Miss Alice] has consummate good taste and great knowledge of plants and flowers.' (This was high praise from the man who had once complained about how overdone everything was at another Rothschild house. After a visit to Halton, his reaction was: 'The showiness! The sense of lavish wealth thrust up your nose.')

On her brother's death, Miss Alice became responsible for the Manor, which meant she spent less and less time at the Pavilion. Then, during the First World War, both Waddesdon and Eythrope gardens were used to grow vegetables to feed the hungry. Even the great parterre at the Manor was dug up to plant potatoes. After the war, as her health declined, Miss Alice lived out the winter months at the Villa Victoria, her property in Grasse, where she made another famous garden, one which cost over half a million pounds a year and needed a hundred gardeners to maintain it. Marcel Gaucher, the son of her head gardener, recalled that every twenty yards a gardener was positioned to catch any leaves that fell. She herself was remembered for always carrying a cane, with a spike on the end for retrieving leaves or cigarette ends. Queen Victoria, a close friend, always called Miss Alice 'the imperious one'. The Queen often visited the Villa in the south of France, but once when she inadvertently stepped over a flower bed, she was roundly reproved for the offence. In later years, her son King Edward VII was similarly ticked off at Waddesdon, when he was told not to touch the furniture.

During Miss Alice's periods at Grasse, she wrote frequently and knowledgeably to her English head gardener, Johnson, instructing him only to grow the best of everything, recommending specific fertilizers, forwarding articles about pests and diseases, telling him which varieties of fruit and vegetables to order, or how many bunches of grapes to send to friends and relations. Her relationship with Johnson was not limited to garden matters. The letters – which are remarkably lively – are equally solicitous about living conditions for gardeners, babies' teething troubles and the importance of rest cures

Haymaking in the meadow in front of the Eythrope garden buildings, in the late nineteenth century.

Miss Alice walking around the parterre pool at the Pavilion.

Miss Alice hosting a tea party at the Pavilion. Baron Ferdinand is seated second from left.

G.F. Johnson, Miss Alice's trusted head gardener and friend.

Mrs James de Rothschild.

after influenza. She also encouraged her head gardener, who spoke French and German as well as English, to keep up with world affairs. As the following letter shows, she wrote to him as a friend with shared interests, rather than as an employee.

Johnson
Send the potatoes as soon as weather permits. The cook can manage for the present.

The "My Magazine" is quite interesting and the short review of the war very good.

A friend writes to me that President Wilson is mediocre and suffers from what the Germans call "Grossenwahn" [delusions of grandeur]. I must say it struck me as a great waste of coal, his being accompanied from the Azores by 20 destroyers.

Poor Clémenceau! I hope he will soon recover – we need him so badly. I am told The Allies are very anxious to get peace signed soon. Battlemania is infecting the army stationed on the Rhine; labour too is very menacing!

I am glad the lad who works for Staunton has a chance of recovering and that Mrs Johnson is better. The weather is lovely here this morning at last!

Miss Alice died in 1922 and both Waddesdon and Eythrope were inherited by her great-nephew, the French James de Rothschild, who, like Baron Ferdinand and his sister, became a naturalized Englishman. He and his young wife – Dorothy, or Dolly – moved into the Manor, and Eythrope was let to tenants. During this period, Miss Alice's garden all but vanished. When James de Rothschild died in 1957, he gave Waddesdon Manor and its estates to the National Trust, with a significant endowment. His widow, who was always known as Mrs James, extended the Pavilion so that she could move to Eythrope. From there she continued to play an important part as chairman of the National Trust's newly formed Management Trust for Waddesdon. Her devotion to the place was admirable, and she loved the garden. Tim Hicks, who worked outside at Waddesdon from the age of fourteen, remembers that they could never shut the glasshouses until 7 p.m., because Mrs James would be enjoying the place until the last of the light faded.

Very little of Miss Alice's ambitious garden remained at Eythrope after it had been let for over thirty years (Victorian gardens were particularly unfashionable after the war), and in the difficult post-war period it was difficult to imagine that high horticulture was ever going to be possible again. But Mrs James did keep the place together, and the best that could be done was done. If Eythrope was to be maintained to traditionally high standards, the place had to be simplified.

When the present Lord Rothschild inherited Eythrope from his cousin Dolly in 1988, he embarked on a huge programme of recreating the past glory of Waddesdon Manor, both in and out of doors, restoring, among many other things, the great parterre that had been grassed over after the war. At the same time, he turned his attention to remodelling Eythrope, where he and his family were to live. The new heir longed to create a garden that would reflect and conserve Miss Alice's high standards in horticulture and it seemed particularly appropriate to do this in the four-acre walled garden, which had once been a perfect example of Victorian productivity. Latterly this area of the garden had been run as a semi-commercial venture. Several greenhouses were in danger of collapsing, sections of wall were missing and the original path layout had vanished. Lord Rothschild's ambition was to create a productive garden that was something like the old Paradise walled garden at Waddesdon.

In 1991 the Rothschilds asked me to design this garden. It was a wonderful commission. At the time I was working on the gardens for the new opera house at Glyndebourne, as well as the gardens at Daylesford House. They were both big projects, but in both cases I was working in collaboration with an architect. Eythrope was different. I knew what was much more important here than the work of any architect or designer was the recruitment of a head gardener who could show real dedication to the meticulously high standards of Miss Alice.

The more I thought about it the more it seemed to me that the gardener who might be ideal was Sue Dickinson. After training at Waterperry, under the legendary Miss Havergal, Sue had worked at Malahide Castle in Ireland, at Kalmthout in Belgium and at Sissinghurst, where she spent three years with Vita Sackville-West's gardeners, Pam Schwerdt and Sibylle Kreutzberger. This was followed by seven years with Esther Merton at Burghfield Old Rectory, which is where I came to know her – as an unparalleled flower gardener. My only anxiety was whether she would be equally interested in growing vegetables. But I did know that her other passion was cooking, and she soon agreed to make a brave commitment to take the job of being in from the beginning. She and I worked together on the layout and setting out of the design (with invaluable technical help from the Waddesdon Clerk of Works, Alan Lesurf). Sue has been the moving spirit behind the garden and her perfectionist zeal and respect for traditional methods is awe-inspiring.

The original brief was that everything outside the walled garden and the area immediately adjoining the house should remain more park than garden. Trees were planted and statues and sculpture added. Lord Rothschild, like his forebears, is a collector, and modern as well as ancient pieces now adorn the grounds.

Near the house, Miss Alice's small parterre was revived as an echo of the great spectacle at Waddesdon. Sue and I spent a long day transferring (with handfuls of sand) the pattern of a design taken from a simple layout shown in Shirley Hibberd's 1871 *The Amateur's Flower Garden* on to a string grid of lines and pegs.

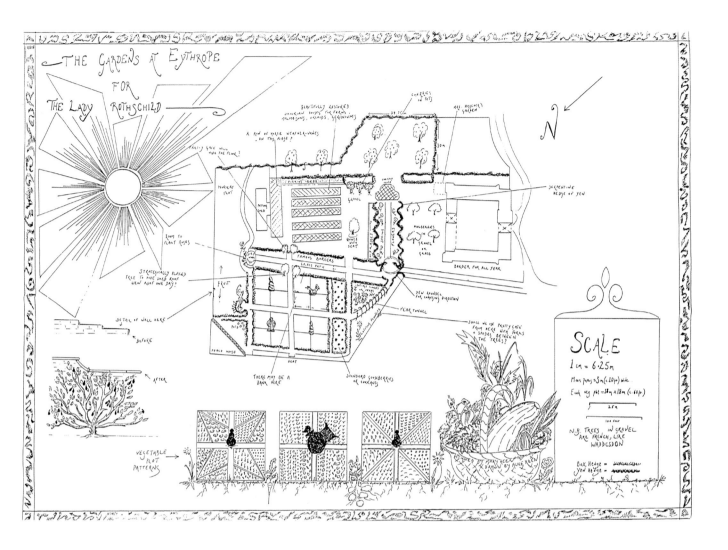

In the new Paradise garden, walls were mended, their heights were rationalized, and then they were topped with tiles to match those on the roof line of the buildings designed by Devey for Miss Alice. This immediately gave the place the distinction it needed. Glasshouses were restored and the traditional layout of four squares divided by paths was reinstated for vegetable growing. Areas were designated for herbs, flowers for cutting, and special collections of plants. The potting shed roof was mended and an orchard was added, as were iron arbours for pears and roses, as well as two herbaceous borders. Lord and Lady Rothschild were interested and involved in the decision-making at every stage.

A quarter of a century later, there are flowers on the terrace and the Pavilion is once again embowered in flowering plants, but the greatest glory of the place is the walled garden of Paradise and plenty. It does all that the Waddesdon Paradise garden did in the way of raising produce, but in addition it doubles as an ornamental garden, with much botanical interest. If Miss Alice were alive today I think even she might be a little imperiously impressed.

Plan for the restoration of the Eythrope garden, designed by Mary Keen and drawn by Alice Keen, 1991.

VEGETABLES

SELF-SUFFICIENCY

Modern gardeners, impelled by the need to save money or by the desire to avoid eating food with an unknown provenance, want to grow their own vegetables. This is a return to what was once normal practice. Until the First World War self-sufficiency was usual, and it was certainly practised by all English estates. The scale of operations in the walled garden at Eythrope may seem daunting to us, but it would have been familiar to many country houses in the nineteenth and early twentieth centuries. And the gardeners of today, however small the plots they have to work, can pick up plenty of ideas and advice from the practice of the gardeners at Eythrope.

It may be disheartening for the average grower to see how healthy and how large are the cabbages that are grown in the walled garden at Eythrope, even in a bad year, but it does bring home the fact that if your only source of supply is what is home-grown, you need to be sure of what you are doing. Conditions vary from place to place and the best way to identify what works in your own particular patch is to write down the timing of operations, so that a pattern of best practice emerges over several seasons. Memory is not always the best way to record what really happened. At Eythrope each of the gardeners keeps a diary, recording in meticulous detail what is sown when and how well it did, and whether this or that variety performed best in a wet summer or a dry one. Weather charts show what actually happened each year, with rainfall and frosts recorded daily.

At Eythrope, hardly any vegetables are bought in, from one year's end to another. Carrots are covered with straw after the first frosts and can be dug until the end of November. Potatoes and onions last beyond Christmas and cabbages and sprouts are still being picked in early February. Celeriac is dug and trimmed, then stored under a straw topping in wooden crates in an open shed. Drumhead and purple cabbages have their outer leaves removed and are then hung from nails in the shed in the dark. Most vegetables are grown only in season, but rocket for winter salads is regularly sown under glass and heads of chicory are forced in the boiler house. In a mild winter, corn salad and the lettuce 'Winter Density' will survive unprotected.

Paul Callingham, whose father, Jack, was head gardener at Eythrope for Mrs James de Rothschild, is now responsible for the vegetable plots. He is proud of what is produced from 2 acres/0.8 hectares of land and how many people it feeds. Apart from the Pavilion, the garden provides for the Dairy at Waddesdon, and baskets of produce are made up for the London house and office, as well as for the family. Guests never leave the place without some seasonal produce in the back of the car. Generosity is in the Rothschild tradition. In a letter to her gardener, Miss Alice wrote, 'Always let me know when you have a lot of ripe strawberries to give away,' and 'Keep the remaining grapes for Christmas and invalids.'

Page 26
Looking over the vegetable plots towards the yard buildings.

Opposite
Seedlings laid out in finely drawn lines, under topiary with a topknot, early in the year.

Opposite
Builders' twine stretched
across posts, ready for
protective netting.

Any surplus vegetables are sold to the Five Arrows pub in the village of Waddesdon, or to the restaurant at the Manor.

Miss Alice displayed remarkable knowledge and interest in her kitchen garden and constantly reminded her head gardener, Johnson, 'I only want the best things grown.' She would instruct him to order a particular French turnip that she had eaten on the Riviera, 'Write to the firm of Vilmorin and ask them for seeds of the white (inside) long shaped variety. I believe they are grown very quickly in very light soil.' But she added the practical caveat 'Of course, if they are not summer vegetables we must do without them.'

At the start of her career as head gardener at Eythrope Sue Dickinson was less used to growing vegetables and fruit than flowers, but she has always been interested in cooking. She made it her business to discover all there was to know about the raising of produce, and more than twenty years into the job she says she is still learning and consulting others who are specialists in a particular crop. Constant revision and experimenting with the way things are grown and new research into varieties for best flavour, or for their keeping qualities, make this a source of invaluable knowledge, as well as reinforcing the best practice of Miss Alice.

One of the earliest visitors to the new regime at Eythrope was Raymond Blanc, who helped with suggestions from tried and tested varieties used at his restaurant at Le Manoir aux Quat' Saisons in Oxfordshire. Since then other vegetables have been trialled in consultation with the Eythrope chef. Small artichokes that can be cooked whole are popular, as they are in Italy, which means growing plenty. Chinese artichokes, which are tiny and fiendish to peel, make good winter soups, as do the knobbly Jerusalem artichokes. Broad beans and peas are picked very young and everybody enjoys masses of asparagus and salads with a variety of leaves. Mangetout peas have been tried but proved less popular than petits pois, which have until recently been hard for the amateur grower to track down. But 'Ceresa' and 'Peawee', which are grown at Eythrope, are now more widely available.

Although the choice of varieties and techniques is innovative, the raised beds that are now so fashionable for edible crops have not been adopted at Eythrope. This is because Sue still thinks that traditional double digging with plenty of manure – as well as home-made compost, plus a top dressing of seaweed in March – is the way to get the best from the ground. The hens in the orchard also contribute to the rich and friable quality of the soil, and the gardeners take it turn to clean the hen houses and add the old bedding to the compost heaps. Keeping poultry is something that is increasingly popular, even with town-dwellers, and chicken manure makes a valuable contribution to any garden; it does, however, need time to rot down, because it is very strong when fresh. Winter digging is a long operation but everyone puts in a stint at digging trenches, an operation to be completed, if possible, before the heavy frosts arrive. If the ground is left roughly dug the weather will finish the work, so that it can be easily rotavated over and broken down in early spring.

Several modern techniques have been adopted in the walled garden. For example, lettuce is always grown from pelleted seed. This is a little more expensive to buy, but saves time on the labour of pricking out and thinning the rows, and it also means there is always a full row of plants. Seedlings do better in jiffy plugs rather than trays. Carrots, beetroot and parsley are sown directly into garden soil. Micromesh, which is used to make a cage for protection from carrot fly, is an innovation that would not have been known to Miss Alice's gardeners. All the brassica crops are protected by gamekeepers' netting, which is supported by stout posts – 1.8 metres/6 feet tall and 90 cm/3 feet round. These are placed 3 metres/10 feet apart. Each post has a nail in the top to secure a length of builders' twine that stretches between the posts. Unlike string, this does not stretch when pulled tight, so the netting never sags. Over each post, the protruding nail is covered by a 12-cm/5-inch clay flower pot, which prevents the netting from getting ripped. It all looks very smart and serviceable and no pigeon can get anywhere near the cabbages. Crops which need picking regularly, like peas, beans and artichokes will have straw spread 10 cm/4 inches deep along the rows where the picker stands, to prevent the soil from getting compacted and feet from carrying too much mud on to the gravel paths. This mulch keeps the soil moist and suppresses weeds. Some wild oats may germinate towards the end of the summer, but that is easily dealt with. Gardeners on heavy soils which compact might try this method and invest in a bale or two of straw. But it is important to remember that as straw – or bark, which is also a good mulch – decomposes, it robs the soil of nitrogen in the process. At the end of the year the straw is dug into the garden to lighten the soil.

Pests and diseases are kept to a minimum by keeping plants well watered and fertilized, but brassicas do get one spray against caterpillars in mid-August. The secret of limiting it to a once-only spray is timing. The best precaution against blackfly, which attacks beans, and flea beetle, which bothers rocket, is to water. Grey aphid, which will ruin lettuces and brassicas in dry conditions, is also controlled by watering. The regular twice-weekly irrigation in the evening with a Rain Bird spray probably also encourages the enormous cabbages. Because the soil is so well prepared, the only additional fertilizer needed is some Vitax Q4 at planting, A seaweed meal dressing is applied in March over the whole garden. This conditions, rather than feeds, the soil and adds trace elements which protect against diseases and are essential for vegetable growing.

The picking and preparing of produce is a time-consuming task. Vegetables are harvested at their freshest. Anyone who has tasted asparagus or new potatoes dug an hour before they are cooked will know how incomparably delicious and sweet they can be. It is up to the gardeners to wash the worst of the mud off any vegetables that are needed, and they are then loaded into blue seed crates and put in the back of the van to be driven up to their various destinations. Eggs, herbs, cut flowers and pot plants are taken on a separate run.

Opposite
Purple cabbages are stored in the dark, hanging from nails on loops of string.

Pages 34 & 39
Winter snow on the pear tunnel and the roofs of the Yard buildings.

Page 35
Cabbages safely netted against pigeons.

Pages 36–37
Strawberries – grown in rotation with vegetable crops – also need protection.

Page 38
Seakale, with the pots removed after forcing.

Pages 40–41
Vegetables, herbs and maidenhair ferns loaded into the van to go up to the house.

SOIL PREPARATION

Preparation of any soil is key to the success of all plants and particularly where vegetables are grown. The ground at Eythrope is heavy clay and hard to work, the kind of soil that is sticky when wet and bone-hard when dry. Many modern vegetable growers who have this problem adopt the raised bed technique, but this is not practised at Eythrope. This may be due in part to the importance attached to the gardening techniques passed down from one gardener to another – as much a conservation exercise here as the garden itself. Whatever the reason, the crops produced at Eythrope after old-fashioned double digging are enviably large, healthy and plentiful. The jury is still out on the benefits of double digging and modern gardeners often prefer methods which rely on building up the soil, rather than digging down. But even the best soil can become compacted at lower depths, and deep digging allows water to filter down and improves the chances of plants taking up nutrients in the upper layer, which they can only do if the soil is moist. Research from the University of Missouri suggests that double digging brings benefits that are worth all the hard work, especially for plants with deeper or tap roots.

The annual dig begins in December, when each of the gardeners will undertake to prepare a patch of ground. In Miss Alice's time, men (and it was all men in those days) dug in lines across the garden. The system now in place is less invidious. Nobody can judge how fast anyone is digging, as they can choose when to tackle their allocated area. In the autumn the garden will have been spread with manure, which keeps the ground workable even in hard frosts. There are four plots each measuring 18 metres/60 feet square to be dug, but only one patch – for the beans – is double dug. The trenches are strips 3 metres/10 feet wide and 75 cm/30 inches long. These are dug two at a time so that the soil from the first spadeful can be set aside to fill the last spit of the second trench beside it. The first spit, a spade's depth and 1.5 metres/5 feet wide, is thrown to the side on the next undug trench then, as the gardener moves down the trench, the topsoil from the next spit is removed and thrown into the first excavation. This is repeated all the way down the trench. Once one length is completed the gardener turns to the second parallel trench and then reverses back down that, filling each spit that is dug with the soil from the one before until reaching the heap of soil from the start of the operation, which has been saved to fill the last hole. If double digging is involved the lower spit, the depth of another spade, is broken up before filling starts, and if manure is added – for the leafy crops that need a rich diet – it goes in before the topsoil. Individual diaries for December record six to eight days when 'continued winter digging' appears. By Christmas it is done. In the spring, the ground will be lightly rotavated and raked to a fine tilth before any sowing can happen.

Opposite
Taking out the first spit of the trench for winter digging.

The spadework starts.

Even in winter this is hot work.

A sharp spade keeps the trench tidy.

Seaweed meal improves the soil.

Rotavating before raking.

Creating a tilth.

Using a string line and a ruled board ensures rows are straight.

The potatoes that are the end result.

Opposite
Spreading compost
and leafmould.

Compost is as critical as digging. There are about six heaps just outside the walled garden. These are defined by wooden posts, with no sides, a method that allows the air to get to the heaps. The heaps, which are 1.8 metres/6 feet square, are piled with garden waste, and a layer of straw is added to every foot of vegetable matter. Mowings are included, but not too many. All garden waste, barring perennial weeds, is destined for compost, as well as vegetable waste from the kitchen at the house, and when the hen houses are cleaned out the manure and shavings are added. Once a heap reaches roughly 1.2 metres/4 feet high, it is shut down with straw. The heaps are never turned, but they rot down of their own accord in a couple of years. The heat generated is not perhaps as high as on some heaps that are managed more scientifically, and Sue worries that not all the annual weed seeds may be sterilized under this more relaxed regime, but the compost looks perfect and in the summer of the second year the heaps provide homes for pumpkins, which are planted in the strawy layer at the top of a finished heap. Then in the autumn, when the fruit is ripe, the compost is ready to be spread around hellebores in the winter beds and roses in the borders.

PEASTICKS AND STAKING

Modern gardeners usually make do with bamboo canes as supports for peas and beans – unless they are lucky enough to find a local supply of the woodland offcuts which were traditionally used in all kitchen gardens. Peasticks and beanpoles cut from coppiced woodland make better stakes than bamboo, because they are easier to manage and look more attractive. For the garden at Eythrope, the props are cut in February, before the sap begins to rise and there is a risk of leaves appearing. Timing is not crucial but dead leaves are unappealing, and it makes sense to do the work when the ground in the garden is still too cold or too wet to be worked.

Four of the gardeners go up into Sheepcote wood, which was planted with an acre of hazels in 1991. The hazel beanpoles cut from this shady area have grown straight and strong. Coppicing is done by cutting out half of the plant every year, using hand tools. This produces 2.4-metre/8-foot beanpoles, as well as 1.8-metre/6-foot benders for training the shrub roses. Any twigs growing off the stem are removed and the ends of the poles are cut into a point, to make them easier to push into the ground.

Although the branches could last for a couple of seasons, they soon start to become brittle. But even at Eythrope, where the local supply is plentiful, the poles are saved for one year in case there are not enough the following year. Once they are no longer needed, they are burnt and the potash from the bonfire is added to the compost heap. (They do also make good seasoned kindling for fires indoors.)

In other woods on the estate, more recent stands of hazel have been planted in less shady places and these, which are coppiced on a three-year rotation, are useful where bushier growth is required. Peasticks must be chosen carefully: they should be bushy at the top where the support will be needed. They need to be shaped at the bottom, using a knife, so that they can be driven into the soil easily, ideally at least 10 cm/4 inches deep. The cut peasticks are tied into manageable bundles and then transported to the working area of the garden behind the potting shed. Twiggy peasticks are needed in 2.4-metre/8-foot lengths for sweet peas, lengths of 1.5–1.8 metres /5–6 feet for herbaceous plants and 1.2-metre/4-foot lengths for the small varieties of peas which are preferred here.

The Waddesdon estate has plenty of places where peasticks and beanpoles can be gathered, but even in medium-sized gardens space can often be found for a row of hazels, which would provide enough support for most purposes. Those who live in rural areas can often get access to woodland where coppicing is practised, as where hazel and birch is grown this is a necessary annual job, to rejuvenate woodland-edge plantings and allow the vital light needed for flora like orchids and bluebells.

Opposite
Runner beans grown on beanpoles gathered from local woods.

Opposite
Beanpoles need to be tall,
as almost 60 cm/2 feet
will be underground
for strength.

In April, when the time comes to use the beanpoles, the ground should be soft enough to push the wood in. If not, it will need soaking. There are always eight beanpoles for each of the twenty-four 3-foot/1-metre square wigwams that fill the designated bean plot each summer. (Sue says that often wigwams are made too narrow, which means they have no stability.) Where the sticks meet, the top of the wigwam is tightly tied with string, wound several times around the crossover neck of the poles. All this is done before any beans are planted.

The first batch of climbing French beans will be sown around the end of April (there will be plenty of other vegetables to eat before they are needed). The little plants go out at the end of May. Self-pollinating runner beans (which are the result of crossing a runner with a French bean) are also sown at the end of May and then more beans are sown in succession every two weeks until the end of June, so that there are enough for five wigwams at a time. Against prevailing advice, true runner beans are sown late. Runners are pollinated by bumblebees and need moisture in the air for a good set, so conditions in September and October are ideal for pollination – and also, from a late sowing, there will be runners to pick until the first frosts. As each crop passes its peak, it is replaced on a fresh wigwam by the latest succession of seedlings. The bean crop is enormous, but it comes at a time when produce is needed and if there is a glut, runner beans freeze well and will be a help in April of the following year, when vegetables are at their scarcest.

As the beans start to grow they may need a little help with clinging to their support until they begin to wind themselves (anti-clockwise) around the props of their own accord. Once the beans are fully grown, there will be no wood visible under the hummocks of green. Gardeners who grow beans in rows – even on stout beanpoles, with transverse supports as I do in my own garden – can find that they are much more susceptible to wind damage that the ones grown on wigwams: this arrangement both provides more support and allows the wind to filter through the gaps between the wigwams. It also means more varieties can be grown.

The peastick operation is slightly different from the beanpole one, because the peas are planted in the ground before the sticks go in. Peasticks, being lighter, are much easier to drive into the ground than the heavier beanpoles, so they go in outside the double row of peas once the seedlings have been hardened off and established for a few weeks in their final planting place. At Eythrope this is usually in April.

Some growers plant their peas in front of netting supported by bamboos, but this leaves them exposed to birds in their early life. If the peas are planted between the rows of sticks, with plenty of twiggy defences at the base, it is harder for pigeons to get near the growing tips, but at Eythrope they are also netted, as jays and partridges as well as pigeons have proved troublesome in the past. If you can do without netting, it makes sense to put in one row of sticks followed by the plants and then to add the outer row.

Carrying the beanpoles.

Trimming off any side growth.

Wigwams are as precisely measured as rows of crops.

Tying the tip firmly.

French beans will be planted here at the end of May.

Making sure sticks are firm.

Twiggy peasticks with the peas between the rows.

At Eythrope, peas are planted in double rows 15 cm/6 inches apart and the bushy sticks are put in on the slant so that they lean against one another for support. With brushwood that is less well branched, they can be either tied together for more strength or woven into a dome. The twigs are very pliable and should easily co-operate. If they do come apart, a little string soon holds them in place. Peas and sweet peas, which are also grown with peasticks, have tendrils that cling to the wood. However, like the climbing beans, they may need a little encouragement at the start, especially if plants are tall when they are first set into the ground. The young shoots are very tender, so tying needs to be carefully done, but the rough surface of the wood is a help to the tendrils because it is much easier to hang on to than slippery bamboo canes which always need more tying in.

Peasticks are also used in the herbaceous borders, among clumps of asters and phlox. The smallest twiggy bits are used in the spring to make a barrier to protect tulips from pheasants in the pear tunnel. Free-range hens (which can do a lot of damage in the garden) can be similarly thwarted.

There is no doubt that native hazel wood is easier on the eye than canes, because it merges into the background as soon as it goes into the ground, which canes will never do.

THE HERB GARDEN

The herb garden in the top south-facing corner of the walled garden contains four beds planted around a medlar tree, with a repeat pattern of edible herbs and annual edible flowers in the middle of the bed.

There is a commonly held belief that herbs are easy to grow and need very little maintenance, but the tastiest herbs come from plants which are constantly reinvigorated. Chives must be divided, thyme and sage clipped neatly and all the leafy herbs need shearing to the ground to keep young growth coming.

An evergreen form of mint selected by the late Tom Harris, who was Professor of Botany at Reading University, is replanted every other year, so that it does not outgrow its space. A few pots are overwintered in the greenhouse so that cuttings can be taken in the New Year.

French sorrel, which has oval leaves and does not run to seed, came from Esther Merton, who brought it home from France in 1950. This can only be propagated from division and needs cutting back to encourage fresh and tender leaves.

French tarragon – rather than Russian tarragon, which is lankier, with an inferior flavor and no scent – is often needed in the kitchen. However, it is not reliably hardy, so cuttings are taken for overwintering under glass.

Two kinds of chives, a particularly large form and a garlic chive, grow in neat rows that edge the paths.

And there are plenty of traditional English herbs. The sage is a form that does not flower and this and the thymes are trimmed early in their life to make neat little buns of growth. Cuttings of the sage are taken in autumn but the common thyme, which has the best flavour for cooking, is renewed from seed, because thyme can succumb to a cold winter if it has been picked too hard. Winter savory also makes a good miniature hedge on the inner circle.

Of the annual herbs, there are two kinds of parsley, the flat-leaf, which the chef likes for flavour, and the curly, which makes the best garnish. Parsley is sown in February under glass for planting out in March and again in July for planting out in September. Since an outbreak of carrot fly it is being grown in the kitchen garden, where it can be rotated, while the herb patch rests until there is no further risk of attack (carrot fly can stay in the ground for a year). The curly parsley grown is 'Bravour', with a deep green colour and long stems which make it easy to bunch, and the flat-leaf is 'Gigante di Napoli' (syn. 'Italian Giant'). Coriander 'Calypso' and dill 'Dukat' (which the chef prefers to fennel) are grown from successional sowings in the salad square in the main part of the kitchen garden.

Marigolds, whose orange petals have been used for seasoning salads and soups since the Middle Ages, add a dash of colour, and there is blue too, from the borage flowers grown for floating in England's traditional summer drink, Pimm's.

Opposite
The herb garden provides edible flowers as well as leaves. Marigolds, nasturtiums and borage are all used in salads.

Curly parsley 'Bravour' is grown for garnishing.

Harvesting sorrel.

Chives – like all the herbs – are cut back regularly.

Harvested crops are carried up to the kitchen in clean trugs.

Basil is grown in pots under glass.

Opposite
Chives, parsley, thyme
and sorrel never reach
flowering stage.

The borage and marigolds are staked with peasticks or they topple over, but canes are used to support the deep purple *Malope* 'Vulcan'. The nasturtium 'Peach Melba', whose peppery leaves and flowers can be eaten, is also grown to add colour to salads.

Some herbs bolt too fast for outdoor sowing. Oregano (sweet marjoram) and chervil, which is another favourite garnish, are grown in succession in punnets in the glasshouse throughout the summer. Basil 'Napolitano' (syn. 'Lettuce Leaf') is never planted out, as summers are rarely warm enough for it to grow well. This is a greenhouse crop, grown in 12-cm/5-inch plastic pots and kept indoors all year. It is hard to harvest, so whole pots go up to the kitchen when they are needed. Once propagating is finished in the spring, half of one greenhouse is dedicated to the basil crop. The smell is wonderful as you step inside.

Like the rest of the kitchen garden, the herb plot is fed with seaweed meal and Vitax Q4 in spring and with Growmore at midsummer. The secret of growing good herbs is constant rejuvenation. This means a practice of cutting down each herb bed in rotation every week throughout the summer – no plant is ever allowed to get woody or seedy. Cutting down does, however, weaken plants, so after this is done they are watered. The midsummer fertilizer also gives them a boost. Fresh herbs are available all year from greenhouse sowings. Coriander, chervil and rocket, which run quickly to seed, are sown in trays every six weeks and pricked out into 9-cm/3½-inch pots of compost made to the John Innes no. 2 recipe but replacing peat with coir. In winter there is a guaranteed supply of mint, parsley, coriander, dill and rocket grown under glass in 12-cm/5-inch pots and kept at a temperature of 5° C/41° F, so that even in the darkest days fresh herbs can be gathered.

PUMPKINS AND SQUASH

Pumpkins and squash are grown for decoration as well as for eating. They make a marvellous display in the Eythope auricula theatre in the autumn, until the first frosts. Sometimes they line the arched entrance passage to the garden, where they are displayed under Alice Oswald's slate poems; and there are always a few on the windowsill in the potting shed. They are a cheerful sight in the dark days.

The chef and Sue have identified the best varieties for cooking, which are mainly the dry orange-fleshed types: butternuts, onion squash 'Uchiki Kuri', 'Buttercup', 'Crown Prince' and pumpkin 'Rouge Vif d'Etampes'. A particular favourite is 'Vegetable Spaghetti' marrow, which turns magically into strands of vegetable pasta when cooked. It tastes delicious with herbs, olive oil and Parmesan, or just with butter and pepper.

All the pumpkins are sown in April under glass in a coir-based John Innes no. 2 compost, mixed with equal parts of coco fibre. The pumpkins and gourds are sown singly in 9-cm/3½-inch plastic pots, with the seed on its side to deter rotting. Once the weather warms up, seedlings will stand outside the greenhouse to harden off for a few weeks, before being planted out at the beginning of June. Many of the more vigorous varieties of the crop are planted on last year's compost heaps behind the frame yard, but a few – the early and most popular varieties like the butternuts 'Hunter' and 'Sprinter' – occupy one square of the vegetable garden. In England, the butternuts are a little harder to grow than the later squashes. They really need a warm climate to do well. Like all the vegetables, the pumpkins will receive a top dressing of seaweed and a helping of Vitax Q4 at the time of planting. Sue finds that the crop is particularly abundant when the pumpkins are grown through mypex, which retain the heat and moisture in the soil below.

In any garden the *Cucurbitaceae* family can be rampant growers when they are planted in the ground. Where space is short it may be easier to grow them on arches, provided there is plenty of support for the plants, as the fruit is heavy – well-grown pumpkins can weigh as much as 4.5 kg/10 lb. The best varieties for arches are probably 'Giraumon Turban' (syn. 'Turk's Turban'), 'Mini Squash' and 'Buttercup'. At Eythrope, the triffid tendency is managed by regular stopping of the growing tips from August onwards. This also encourages the fruit to set, so that luscious and beautiful pumpkins and squash can be harvested by the end of September. In a good year, as many as two hundred might be collected.

Pumpkins, squashes and gourds do not last well after frosts. Butternuts keep best if harvested and brought indoors to finish at a temperature of 20°C/68°F for a fortnight to harden the skins. At Eythrope they come into one of the glasshouses, but a warm windowsill would be just as good. Once the skins are hard, the pumpkins and spaghetti marrow will keep until Christmas in a frost-free shed.

Opposite
Once harvested, the fruits need to be dried out before being stored. The cherry house provides a useful drying area.

Pages 66–67
The auricula theatre is used for a late display of pumpkins and squashes.

Labelling pots.

Seeds are sown on their sides to prevent rotting.

One label for each tray is enough.

The compost heap provides the perfect home for pumpkin seedlings.

They must be firmly planted.

Even in a compost heap, rows should be neat.

Growing conditions are ideal.

By late summer the heap is covered with leaves.

FRUIT

GROWING FRUIT

Before the days of worldwide transport and home freezers, when all country estates aimed to be self-sufficient, head gardeners took a special pride in growing perfect fruit. The skill and cost of producing such perfection was a good excuse for display. Victorian country house tables often used fruit as decoration and it was a matter of honour to bring fruit to the table weeks before it ripened outside. Producing grapes all year round was a particular strength of the Victorian head gardener and there was intense rivalry over who grew the best bunches. (The Dukes of Devonshire and Marlborough still compete annually at the Royal Horticultural Society show for who grows the best Muscat grapes under glass.)

During the reign of Miss Alice, nobody could outdo the Rothschilds for the high standards that prevailed throughout the gardens at Waddesdon and Eythrope, and when writing to her gardener from France it was the fruit that she mentioned most. She wrote of French pear varieties tasting better than English ones, of plums needing to be watered with chalky water, and enclosed recent articles about blackcurrant diseases or recipes for home-made fertilizers. Still today the fruit that comes to the dining room in the Pavilion, or to a gala dinner at the Manor, is perfect in appearance as well as taste.

All the usual soft fruits are grown in the walled garden, but the varieties chosen are those which tend only to be well grown in a private garden. Supermarket strawberries and raspberries are developed more for their keeping qualities than for their flavour. The strawberry 'Mara des Bois', which has a long fruiting season and tastes faintly scented, like an alpine strawberry, is never available from a shop. There are true alpine strawberries, 'Baron Solemacher', 'Alexandra' and 'Mignonette', which all take an age to pick. 'Glen Ample' is a dependable summer raspberry, and the varieties chosen for autumn fruiting seem to do particularly well: they include a new variety, 'Joan J', with fruit the size of thimbles and no spines on the canes, as well as the reliable 'Autumn Bliss'. The raspberry season lasts from July until October and the fruit is never netted, as there are enough berries to feed birds as well as people (happily, the birds seem less keen on autumn than summer varieties). The canes are mulched with leafmould: this makes the soil more acid, which suits raspberries. Trace elements for all the fruit are provided by a dressing of Vitax Q4 in the spring. There are bushes of red- and blackcurrants and gooseberries for cooking, as well as for dessert. The best gooseberry for eating, in Sue's opinion, is 'Pax' and a good heavy cropper for cooking is 'Invicta'. Both of these modern varieties are more resistant to mildew than older types.

Plums, greengages, the 'Oregon Thornless' blackberry and a few dessert apples are grown as cordons or fans or espaliers on the walls that contain the kitchen garden. (Cordons are a good way of maximizing the use of space and are useful in small gardens, where they can be trained against fences as well as walls.) There are apples

Page 68
Apple 'Court Pendu Plat'.

Opposite
A bunch of the dessert grape 'Schiava Grossa' (syn. 'Black Hamburg'), grown under glass.

Opposite
Plums are so heavy that
a good crop can break
the branches of the tree.
Growing them against
a wall provides
additional support.

Pages 74 & 79
The pear tunnel (where
apple trees also grow) in
winter. Hazel sticks in
the ground protect tulip
bulbs from pheasants.

Page 75
Apple 'Cox's Orange
Pippin'.

Pages 76–77
The pear tunnel
in summer.

Page 78
Apple 'Cornish
Gilliflower'.

and pears trained over the iron arbour tunnel, with outdoor grapes twined where the arches cross and flowers beneath the fruit to line the paths. The blossoming fruit above tulips in boiled sweet colours makes a dazzling spring display, while in winter the structure of the well pruned trees creates a telling architectural feature. On either side of the pear tunnel, the small lawns are planted with quince trees, which bear masses of heavy golden fruits in October. Their scent is one of the pleasures of the autumn kitchen and one quince is enough to transform the taste of cooked apples into something ambrosial.

The orchard at Eythrope has the large variety of apples that Jean Claudius Loudon, the Alan Titchmarsh of Victorian times, recommended in order to spread the season from August to June the following year. Arranged in boxes and labelled they are displayed for a weekend or two under the arched passage that leads to the garden, so that gardeners and interested guests can learn to tell one apple from another.

The trees are spaced 6 metres/20 feet apart, which is generous, and grown as half-standards, which are much easier to pick than the huge traditional forms that would have prevailed in Loudon's day. Large cookers that foam into a pulpy mass were Loudon favourites and Sue thinks that 'Peasgood's Nonsuch' and 'Reverend W. Wilkes', which satisfy this criterion, are two of the best for eating, as well as for cooking to a froth with very little sugar. Russet apples are especially popular and several of these were added five years after the orchard was planted in 1991. The centre of the apple trees is kept open. (Old growers always claimed that you should be able to throw a hat through the branches of an apple tree.) Under the trees, the house flock of chickens runs free. The Burford Browns, which lay delicious brown eggs, peck about in the orchard grass but must spend the night indoors if they are to defeat the ever-watchful fox. Foxes can also be fearless by day, but there are usually enough people in the garden to prevent daylight robbery.

Growing fruit under glass was once a feature of all grand kitchen gardens, and at Eythrope there are separate houses for cherries, Muscat grapes, apricots and figs. Until 2012 there was a peach case in the angle of the walls at the back of the pot garden, but it collapsed and was deemed too far gone to be rescued, so peaches and nectarines now share the cherry house. Pineapples are not grown at Eythrope now (although a famous variety available in Miss Alice's day was 'Charlotte de Rothschild', which was prized more for table decoration than flavour).

The fig house is damped down several times a day and, although it is not heated, the steamy scent of figs in summer is strangely exotic. None of the fruit grown under glass at Eythrope needs heating: owners of a greenhouse that has become too expensive to keep frost-free might consider using it to raise fruit under cover. The added protection ensures better ripening, but all fruit grown under glass will need careful ventilation and watering, as well as meticulous observation, so that any troubles can be dealt with before they turn into major problems. Vines grown in unheated houses are much more subject to botrytis than those where a little heat is enjoyed. If no sprays are used on the fruit, constant vigilance is vital. For stone fruit, the timing of watering also matters.

CHERRIES IN POTS

The most remarkable task in the garden, and that demanding the most dedication, involves the growing of dessert cherries in pots in what is now called the cherry house. The restored octagonal house where they grow was once the rose house, but when the cherry house at the Manor was demolished in the 1950s some of the trees that were grown there were brought down to the gardens at Eythrope.

When Sue took over the garden she inherited a wealth of knowledge from Jack Callingham. He was then at the end of his working life as head gardener, but he taught her what he had learned from Miss Alice's gardener, Mr Johnson, whose apprentice he had been in the early years of the twentieth century. This detailed information was never written down, but was passed verbally from generation to generation of gardeners. A few methods might be adjusted, but the principles are the same as they were in Miss Alice's day.

Cherry trees of four different varieties – 'Napoleon', 'Early Rivers', 'Hedelfingen Riesenkirsche' (syn. 'Géant d'Hedelfingen') and 'Merton Glory') are grown in 60-cm/2-foot clay pots, with feeding collars. This is an old technique used by the nineteenth-century fruit grower Thomas Rivers. The trees spend the winter outdoors, but are carried into the cherry house in February, when the old feeding collars are removed. New collars are then shaped from equal parts of molehill loam and strawy manure, which must be moulded and mounded around the inside of the pot. The roots of the trees creep into the collars (which make a saucer around the edge of the pot) so that water and feeds can be more efficiently applied. Once this is done, a top dressing of seaweed fertilizer and Vitax Q4 is applied. (The cherries used to be fed with manure water made from a sack of sheep droppings, but this process proved too horrible to endure.)

There is no heat in this greenhouse, where peaches and nectarines are trained round the sides, and in March the vents must be closed at night to force the cherry trees into early blossom. Once the blossom forms, the flowers must be pollinated, but because there are very few insects around at this time of year, pollination has to be done artificially. Cross-pollination between varieties is critical at this stage. This is done every day at 12 noon, using a rabbit's tail (but a squirrel paintbrush would do as well). After pollination the floor is damped down to achieve the right atmosphere for fertilization to take place.

Once the fruit has set, in April, the greenhouse must be kept cool for the cherries to form their stones so, if the weather warms up, the vents are kept open day and night. Watering must be precise. If the pots are allowed to dry out entirely and are then given a lot of water, the fruit will split; but too much water will drown the roots. So the balance is critical. In addition, limey water, rather than rainwater, must be used once a week to help the cherries form their stones. Once the stones have set and the fruit begins to swell, a weekly high-potash liquid feed is added.

Opposite
Ripe 'Early Rivers' cherries.

Old feeding collars on trees newly brought into the cherry house.

The old collar is carefully removed.

Sacking around the base catches any manure that falls.

The new collar is moulded from a mix of manure and molehill soil.

The collar is built up in layers.

The collar will keep the tree roots fed and watered for a season.

Any splashes of dirt are brushed off with a wet brush.

Each tree is labelled with the name of the variety.

Opposite
The cherry trees in blossom in the cherry house. The gardeners tap the pots with the boxwood hammer to test whether the soil is damp enough. A ringing sound means watering is needed.

Pages 86–87
'Napoleon' cherries ripening on the trees.

At this point the cherries should start to look shiny; if they turn yellow and begin to wither they will never mature properly and will soon drop off the tree.

In such large pots it is hard to judge whether enough water has been applied. The best way to tell if more water is needed is by tapping the pot with a small hammer made out of boxwood. A dull sound means the soil is damp enough, but if the hammer makes a ringing noise like a bell, it is time to water.

If the sun is hot the greenhouse must be damped down three times a day, starting with a flick of the hose over the trees before midday. (Luckily the same regime suits the peaches and nectarines growing round the edges of the cherry house.) Dry air encourages pests – blackfly and red spider mite can attack at any time – so vigilance is vital, and whoever is on duty at weekends must observe the same daily routine. The new shoots of the cherry trees must be pinched back to three buds to discourage infestations of blackfly, which tend to congregate on the growing tips. If any trees do get attacked, the fruit must be stripped: spraying is never an option. Pinching out the growing tips also ensures that the trees do not get too large.

Picking starts at the end of May and goes on until mid-July. In a good year (which means a cool spring, as we had after the cold April of 2013), each tree will yield 3.5–4.5 kg/8–10 lb of fruit, which goes indoors to be beautifully arranged on Meissen or silver plates. In the best tradition of Miss Alice, baskets of cherries in season are sent as presents to friends, especially to those visiting from abroad.

Once the season is over in mid-July, the trees spend the rest of the year outside in their pots until February of the following year, when the whole process is begun all over again. But in order to keep them in pots they must be pruned in late summer: this is done by again stopping each shoot to three or four buds.

APPLES AND PEARS

When the first National Apple Conference was held in 1883 at Chiswick – where the Royal Horticultural Society was then based – it was an indication of how important the apple had become to Victorian gardeners. Over a thousand varieties were put on display and of these many had been bred by the head gardeners of country house estates.

By that time it was possible to grow a dessert apple that was fit to eat for over six months of the year. British appetites and the temperate climate have always been well suited to apples. In the early years of the twentieth century, the nurseryman and apple expert Edward Bunyard wrote, 'No fruit is more to our English taste than the Apple. Let the Frenchman have his Pear, the Italian his Fig, the Jamaican may retain his farinaceous Banana and the Malay his Durian, but for us the Apple'.

Apples grown either as espaliers to line the paths of kitchen gardens or fan-trained on walls would have been a feature of the Waddesdon Paradise garden. After Mrs James moved to Eythrope she continued to be proud of the fruit that was grown in the garden, and the legacy of her apples remains on some of the walls. The fan-trained 'Holstein' (a Cox from the early years of the twentieth century) and 'Discovery' (a much more recent – 1948 – introduction) were both planted by Jack Callingham, head gardener to Mrs James and father of Paul, who is now in charge of the vegetables.

The pear tunnel actually has alternate rows of cordon or single stem apples, as well as pears, and these have been chosen from some varieties that Miss Alice would certainly have known. They have also been selected for their blossom. 'Irish Peach' is a very early dessert apple which was introduced in 1820. Like the modern early eating apple 'Discovery', it does not keep, but – again like 'Discovery' – it has the most beautiful blossom. 'Brownlee's Russet' is another Victorian apple that grows on the tunnel arches and this has blossom of deepest pink. In small gardens, apple trees, in whatever form they are grown, will earn their keep by the beauty of their blossom as well as the fruit they produce.

The orchard has several other old varieties but these are grown as half-standard trees rather than the full standard height, because half-standards are so much easier to pick and to prune. Many of the orchard apples, especially the old-fashioned types like 'Lord Derby' and 'Newton Wonder', are used for cooking. But 'Newton Wonder' is also a good dessert apple if it is kept. A little-known 1920 dessert apple is 'Chivers Delight', which was bred for bulking up jam, but turns out to be easy and delicious. 'Orleans Reinette' is another favourite eating apple. The fruit is stored for eating in trays in cool sheds so that it lasts all winter. In the past apple juice has also been a great success. The dessert apple season starts in August with 'Discovery' and 'Irish Peach' and ends in April with 'Tydeman's Late Orange'.

Opposite
The spring blossom of 'Brownlee's Russet' apple.

Pruning orchard trees with a long-handled saw.

Pears on the arches are spurred back.

Tip-pruning orchard apples.

Pruning tools ready in a trug.

Apple trees need to have space between their branches.

Pears, too, have been chosen for their historic interest and desirable blossom. The French pear 'Catillac', which also grows on the tunnel, was eaten at the court of Louis XIV. This has the largest blossom of any pear, as well as the largest fruit. A single pear can weigh as much as 2 pounds, or almost a kilogram. This is a fruit to poach rather than eat raw. (Even if it had been edible raw, it would have been considered unseemly to eat anything so large in Miss Alice's day, when it was not acceptable to halve a fruit and share it with another at the table, so small apples and pears were always preferred.)

Other Victorian pears grown on the iron arches are 'Williams' Bon Chrétien' a nineteenth-century pear, and 'Doyenné du Comice', a mid-nineteenth-century introduction from France, as well as the versatile 'Conference', which was in circulation by 1880. 'Beth' and 'Concorde' are more modern. Sue suggests that where there is room for only one pear, the variety to choose is 'Concorde' – a dessert pear bred by crossing 'Comice' and 'Conference'– because it is self-fertile and never develops scab.

Restricted forms such as fans, espaliers or cordons trained over arches can deliver higher-quality fruit than free-standing trees. Grown against a wall, a dessert apple or pear benefits from all the available light and warmth. Restricting the growth of leaves concentrates the energies of the bush on producing fruit, so that flavour is better and fruits tend to be larger. (However, tip-bearing apples are not suitable for growing as restricted forms.) Once the initial shape of the tree has been built up by winter pruning, fan-trained and cordon fruits are pruned in August, when growth has slowed down. All the side shoots from the main branches are reduced to about 7.5 cm/3 inches and any that grow again will be cut back a second time in September. The 'June drop' is the natural way that apple trees thin their own fruit, but fruit trained to walls is less likely to be exposed to wind. If the crop is heavy, fruit thinning must be done manually, and this will mean better-quality fruit in the autumn, as well as a better chance of fruit the following year. The enormous annual crop of apples and pears at Eythrope is evidence that this system delivers delicious fruit as well as attractive garden features.

APRICOTS

Apricots, peaches and nectarines involve a lot of work. They can be grown outside on a warm wall, but at Eythrope they are grown as fan-trained trees in cold glasshouses. All of them will produce fruit on wood made the previous season, so they need careful pruning and tying in during the winter and this must be finished well before the buds start to develop early in the New Year. Apricots have additional requirements, because they also form fruit on short spurs of older wood, so they are pinched back first to three leaves and then a second time, about three weeks later, to one leaf. At Eythrope the apricots are pruned on the spur system (leaving the main shoots and pinching out the side shoots or spurs). Ideally all this is done with finger and thumb. Reducing the height of the main stems is often done in August and tying in of new shoots to make the fan shape happens as shoots grow, but at Eythrope all this is done in winter, with some thinning of shoots in summer.

Apricots are vigorous. They need a wall at least 2.4 metres/8 feet high and will occupy about 4.5 metres/15 feet of space. 'Moor Park' and 'New Large Early' are both old varieties and in a good summer each tree may bear as much as 55 kg/120 lb of fruit. Many growers thin their fruit, but this is not done at Eythrope; some fruit does drop of its own accord.

The blossom is hand-pollinated each midday with a rabbit's tail on a stick. If the air is dry trees will need misting, and the roots of the tree should never be allowed to dry out. (Miss Alice knew the value of chalky water for plums, and all stoned fruits do better on limy soil.) However, overwatering can be equally damaging. Apricots need plenty of ventilation and they also resent being forced. Scale insects can be a nuisance and spraying with soft soap solution or a pyrethrum-based insecticide may be needed. Fruit is usually ready to pick in August and it can be frozen for cooking through the winter.

Opposite
Apricot 'Moor Park'.

BLACKBERRIES

Cultivated blackberries are a far cry from the prickly tangle that bursts from the hedgerows. It may seem ridiculous to give garden room to a plant which is found everywhere in the wild and can be picked for free, but there is a huge difference between improved and unimproved varieties. The garden berries are larger, more delicious and juicier, with fewer seeds, and they are much more abundant. One trained bush of the 'Oregon Thornless' blackberries grown at Eythrope will produce as much as 10 kg/22 lb of berries a year. If the bushes are watered copiously once a fortnight, as the berries begin to redden, the fruit will be even larger.

The usual spread of a cultivated blackberry is almost 3 metres/10 feet, so the bushes need plenty of space. Provided there is a framework of wires about 30 cm/1 foot apart on the wall, the canes can be trained in any number of ornamental ways. At the beginning of summer the blackberry bushes on the walls at Eythrope are so exquisitely arranged that they might have no other point than to be decorative. However, the summer growth needs tying in as the canes grow, and as they are very vigorous this necessitates regular attention. While the fruit on the current summer's shoots is ripening, the canes that will carry next year's berries will also be shooting up. These can be bundled together to give the current crop the best chance of ripening. Once the fruit is picked the old canes can be cut down and the new ones trained to take their places. Although blackberries do fruit on two-year-old canes the crop will never be as plentiful as on the newer ones.

Opposite
The 'Oregon Thornless' blackberry bushes in the walled garden start the summer as a well-organized pruned arrangement, but grow fast and wild until the fruit is borne.

Pruning 'Oregon Thornless' blackberries.

Growth is vigorous.

Strong shoots are temporarily tied in.

The ultimate layout and spacing are arranged with precision.

FIGS AND VINES

The figs at the end of the vine house at Eythrope are scions of the figs Miss Alice grew at Grasse. Cuttings of the French fruit were brought to Waddesdon and grown there, and then when Mrs James moved to the Pavilion a row of cuttings was planted in the greenhouse bed at Eythrope. This multi-stemmed unnamed fig is not grown, as most figs are, from a single trunk; instead, the shoots are fan-trained and tied to wires under the roof so that it has the appearance of being a single tree. The glasshouse is unheated, but in England all figs do need some protection from frost to guarantee an abundant crop the following summer.

If they are to fruit well figs must be restricted, as their tendency is to grow too vigorously. Pruning their roots can help to control growth and traditionally they are planted next to a wall and grown in the poorest stony soil available. At Eythrope the roots are contained in a bed and no fertilizer is added. Pruning of branches must be equally rigorous so as to concentrate the energy of the tree into producing the short jointed annual shoots which fruit at their tips the following summer. These need to ripen before the winter if they are going to be strong enough to bear the figs, so it is important to reduce any leaves and shoots which will interfere with their access to light and warmth.

The time to start keeping the productive stems clear of the rest is before the sap rises. Anything that is likely to crowd the shoots that are emerging must be taken out and tied in. Outside, the growth spurt may start a little later. Under glass this is completed before Christmas. Some fruits develop in the axils of the leaves, and out of doors these will never ripen in the same year and will not overwinter, so they need to be removed. The ones that are borne on the tips of the foot-long shoots made and ripened the previous summer will always be the most productive source of fruit, both in and out of doors. At Eythrope the new shoots are spurred back in May or June to two-thirds of their length – usually four buds – and tied in. Any later growth is reduced to two buds. Some people develop a rash from the drops of sap that can fall from the cut ends of the fig, so pruning is always done from the base of the tree upwards. Figs grown outside will need pinching back to the fifth leaf around the end of August and any small figs that form near the base of the shoot have to be removed, so that the tiny ones at the tips can develop and overwinter and ripen the following year. Under glass two crops of figs can be enjoyed. The overwintered ones which would not survive a winter outside will be ready to eat in August and the smaller tip-borne ones will follow in September.

Figs need to be kept damp while they are growing and the bitter green smell of their leaves as you wander through the closed fig house is strangely exotic. By the end of August the fruits will be ready to pick, but they are always left to ripen on the tree until they start to split a little.

Opposite
A scion of Miss Alice's fig from Grasse.

Opposite
Vines trained on the
roof supports, with
pelargoniums below.

Vines were another speciality of Miss Alice's. In her day they were stored until Christmas, when she issued instructions about sending bunches to friends and dependants. 'Arrange with Sims to send three bunches with his turkey to Miss Phipps; send one bunch to Mrs Adcock to Brighton, send 4 bunches to Mrs Watkin and one for Miss Wadham at Streatham' were her orders to head gardener Johnson in 1905.

In the twenty-first-century garden there is a 'Schiava Grossa' from Hampton Court, a 'Muscat of Alexandria' from Chatsworth and another Muscat which came from Waddesdon. Head gardeners in such places took time and trouble to grow grapes to perfection. But the vine house at Eythrope is minimally heated in comparison with the way it would have been kept at Waddesdon, which means there is more risk of mildew. Ventilation must be managed carefully and the windows are open all winter so that the buds stay dormant in January and February while there is still a risk of frost. At the end of February the heat is put on to 10°C/50°F to start the vine rods into growth. If it is sunny and the temperature rises too much the house must be kept damp, but by nightfall, or on cloudy days, the atmosphere should be dry.

Once new growth has started, the shoots are reduced to two to each spur and tied in to the wires above them, spaced about 30 cm/1 foot apart. When flowering begins the temperature can be allowed to rise but ventilation is still important, even at night. Pollination is done by tapping the vines at midday and by running both hands down a flowering bunch. As the bunches form, any poor-looking ones will be removed. The ideal is that on each rod of the vine the grapes should be set at 30 cm/1 foot spacing. When the grapes swell they must be thinned with scissors. This is fiddly work and needs sharp eyes, as all the seedless berries must be removed. As a rough rule, 'Schiava Grossa' will lose two berries in every three at this stage. The Muscats are trickier to set fruit, so they are thinned less. But all thinning in the bunches must be done before the grapes have swollen to their full size, as then the task becomes impossible. While the fruit is ripening the house needs to be kept damp, especially in sunny weather, and any new growth from the fruiting shoots will need removing if it occupies too much space.

In an unheated house grapes can hang on the vines until October. When the temperature drops to below 10°C/50°F they are removed and the house can then be allowed to cool, with plenty of ventilation, so that the leaves drop and the vines go into dormancy. As soon as the leaves are down, before Christmas, all the side shoots are pruned back to two buds (any sublaterals are removed completely) and the rods have their tips lowered to the ground. In January the top 5 cm/2 inches of soil in the bed is removed, so that vines can be top-dressed with John Innes no 2. The front of the border is lightly forked, then leafmould, Vitax Q4 and seaweed meal are added and the bed is watered.

The work of scraping the bark off the rods starts after Christmas and must be finished by the end of January. This is a time-consuming task, but it is still the best way of dealing with mealy bug, which can hide under old bark. A knife is used to remove the silvery bark but it should not damage the green layer below.

The tools for the job of training figs: just scissors and string.

Appearance is important: knots are kept neat.

The figs are trained to wires beneath the roof.

Branches are close to one another.

The fruit will not be ready to eat until it splits open.

GLASSHOUSES

GROWING UNDER GLASS

Before the glass tax was abolished in 1845, only the grandest estates could afford to raise fruit and exotic plants in greenhouses. Once more modest establishments could afford to build glasshouses, country houses doubled and trebled the size of their glass and Eythrope was no exception. An article about the Pavilion in the *Bucks Herald* in 1890 described 'three span roofed structures each a hundred feet long by eighteen feet wide, erected by Messrs Halliday of Manchester and admirably adapted for plant culture.' These are no longer in the garden, but the 'five other span roofed houses, ninety feet long by fourteen foot wide, devoted to propagation purposes', were still standing in 1990, when the present Lord Rothschild took over the estate. These sunk pit houses with fine slate floors and benches were in sad need of restoration and this was one of the first garden tasks to be tackled. The broken houses were mended with wood and painted white, but after three years, when the cost of repainting and keeping the wood going proved prohibitive, the decision was taken to replace the structures with modern aluminium. Alitex extruded aluminium mouldings from the wood, reused all the winding gear and fittings and kept the slate floors, so that only a very keen eye can tell the difference between ancient and modern. The maintenance of these is minimal. They are heated by oil-fired boilers and each house has two or three climate zones and provides several crops a year. It is here that all the propagating for bedding plants and vegetables takes place. The chance to grow everything needed for the gardens for bedding displays, cut flowers, pot plants for house decoration, as well as vegetables and fruit, is rare these days. In the autumn, propagation from cuttings for all the summer bedding takes a total of six weeks for two gardeners. After Christmas more bedding plants and cut flowers are raised from seed. Each year, techniques for raising plants from seed or cuttings are refined in the light of experience.

There is a house dedicated to tomatoes and cucumbers and another to the geraniums (pelargoniums) that are used in bedding schemes or for the many decorating needs in various Rothschild family houses. The pelargonium house was apparently a feature in 1890, when the ivy leaf 'Souvenir de Charles Turner' was admired by the writer of the *Bucks Herald* article. Three hundred of the Victorian geraniums 'Paul Crampel' and 'Crystal Palace Gem' are raised annually for bedding at the front of the Pavilion and seven hundred 'Lady Ilchester' and 'Lady Plymouth' are grown for the parterre. In Miss Alice's day there were plenty of orchids. These are no longer grown at Eythrope but the Malmaison carnations which she loved are still grown under glass. In the late nineteenth century there were a thousand Malmaisons at Eythrope, and today half of one house is still dedicated to these pampered and demanding flowers.

Page 106
The entrance to the glasshouses, with the pool in front.

Opposite
Cucumbers are trained on frames to the apex of the house.

Opposite
Onions drying out in a
pit house that is
empty for summer.

Pages 112–113
Eric Ravilious, *The
Greenhouse: Cyclamen
and Tomatoes*, 1935,
watercolour. The
arrangement of the
tomatoes grown at
Eythrope is based on
this painting.

Pages 114 & 119
Tomatoes in pots, with
the canes that will
support them.

Page 115
Beef tomatoes are
useful for stuffing.

Pages 116–117
Meticulous training
provides a summer
feast for the eye as well
as for the kitchen.

Page 118
Pepper 'Nardello'.

As well as the five pit houses, a vinery and fig house, the cherry house and a smaller greenhouse now dedicated to auriculas were all restored. Sadly the peach case on the south-facing wall was demolished in 2012, but peaches, nectarines and apricots are still grown in the cherry house.

In Victorian gardens, according to the kitchen garden expert Susan Campbell, the glasshouse was the realm of the head gardener and perhaps his second in command. Outdoor workers never set foot in the prized glass temples to horticulture. These days each member of the Eythrope team is responsible for one of the houses, and they all share the work of weekend watering, ventilating and damping down. All this is done three times a day in each house during the summer months, to reduce the risk of pests. There is always the buoyant atmosphere of healthy plants and the succession of smells of scented-leaf geraniums, ripe tomatoes, heliotropes and large-leaf basil plants as you step down to walk through one after another of the glazed rooms is thrilling.

Not an iota of space is wasted. Under the staging, clivias and ferns are packed in pots and in summer onions will be left to dry in an empty zone. The crops change in the five pit houses in May after the heating is turned down to 0°C/32°F at the end of April. Only the middle section of the propagating house (number 1) is kept at 15°C/60°F all year. In October there is another crop change, when the heating is turned on for the winter. Shading is painted on the houses in April and is removed at the end of September.

TOMATOES, PEPPERS,
AUBERGINES AND CUCUMBERS

It was not until Miss Alice's day that tomatoes really began to be appreciated as a food. *Beeton's Garden Management*, published in 1870, says that not only is the tomato useful for an 'admirable sauce', 'it also may be cooked and brought to the table like other vegetables, in several different ways; or eaten raw cut into slices like cucumber, but much thicker, and dressed with salt and pepper, oil and vinegar in the same way. Further, it is extremely palatable when eaten as a fruit, dipped in sugar. Those who have analysed its properties say that the tomato is singularly wholesome, still, it is not appreciated or cultivated as it ought to be.'

At Eythrope in the twenty-first century, tomatoes are grown in abundance in two sections of greenhouse number 5 and half of number 3. They are never planted outside, because English summers are rarely hot enough to ripen them and the risk of blight in rainy seasons is too great. Blackbirds can also damage outdoor tomatoes. The glass will be unheated as the boilers are switched off by May. Where warmer conditions are needed (for aubergines or cucumbers), this can be arranged by keeping the house less ventilated.

Sowing of the many different varieties is dictated by how much space is available, and summer bedding takes priority over other propagation. The first sowing of the cherry types destined for greenhouse number 3 starts at the end of February, when a few of the black Russian variety 'Black Krim' are also sown. By the end of March, 'Ferline' and 'Fantasio', which have become the standard reds grown for flavour, will be sown, and a few last sowings of other varieties will take place in the first week of April. Forty 'Ferline' and 'Fandango' will fill the whole of the first section of number 5 and the 'experimentals' will be grown in the second section. The early sowing will be potted on into 9-cm/3½-inch pots at the beginning of April. A month later they will be moved into 12-cm/5-inch pots in the standard soil mix and then by the end of May they will be ready to move into their final destination, a 25-cm/10-inch whalehide pot. In each pot a cane tall enough to reach the roof arch will be inserted, so that the stems can be tied to these and grown as single cordons. This beautiful arrangement is inspired by the 1935 Eric Ravilious watercolour painted at Firle House in Sussex. Some twenty varieties – a total of seventy plants – will be raised under glass to be used all summer for salads and tomato juice as well as for cooking. The side shoots are pinched out regularly, as well as some of the lower leaves, because doing this allows air to circulate and prevents aphid attacks. A weekly feed of a high-potash fertilizer is vital once the fruit starts to set and watering is done from a hose, with a lance on the end. The tomatoes are usually cleared by the last week of September.

Opposite
All the cucumbers grown are varieties of self-pollinating F1 female hybrids.

121

Aubergine 'Moneymaker No. 2' is sown early, around the end of February, because it needs a long growing season. The aubergines follow the same progression as the tomatoes, from 9-cm to 12-cm to 25-cm whalehide pots, and move into their separate high-humidity section of the number 1 house. Flowering usually starts in July. Ideally the blossom is fertilized by the increasingly rare bumble bee, but if the bees fail there is some help at hand from a sable paintbrush. The aubergines are grown as bushes, which do not need training, but sometimes if the fruit becomes too heavy the laterals will require support. Greenfly and whitefly can be a problem, but this is controlled by a soft-soap spray and by occasional visits from hoverflies. The feeding and watering regime is the same as for tomatoes and, as in all the greenhouses, the floor is damped down three times a day. Watering is one of the hardest things to judge for any greenhouse plant. Most people, lacking the experience of the Eythrope gardeners, tend to overwater, which attracts sciarid fly; underwatering, on the other hand, can encourage whitefly. As a rough guide, proper watering should fill the top 1.25 cm/½ inch of a pot above the soil.

Sweet peppers are another glass crop. Those grown are mainly – though not exclusively – the longer-fruited kinds. Capsicums are sown towards the end of March and like the tomatoes and aubergines will end up in 25-cm whalehide pots after being moved on from smaller plastic pots. They do best in a drier atmosphere than the aubergines, and will fill the middle section of number 1. Peppers are self-pollinating and do not need training, but their brittle stems cannot support too much weight, so there will be some thinning of fruit on the lateral stems. Once the flowers and fruit begin to show, they will be given a weekly feed of high-potash fertilizer.

Cucumbers are sown in early March and again in April and the varieties chosen are all self-pollinating female F1 hybrids. They are grown separately, in the third section of the number 5 house (tomatoes occupy the other two zones), but they need less ventilation and a more humid atmosphere than tomatoes. The cucumbers follow the same potting routine as the other glasshouse vegetables and are restricted to two leading shoots, supported by a cane to the height of the roof ridge and then on down to the opposite bench. Their weekly feed is a liquid high-nitrogen fertilizer, rather than the potash mix that is given to the other crops.

Shoots in the armpits of tomato plants are taken out.

Some leaves are removed to let in extra light.

Stems are tied to the canes as they grow.

Knots are trimmed so that they hardly show.

Tomatoes lined up in their 25-cm/10-inch whalehide pots.

PELARGONIUMS

'Few people know, before they try, what it is to fill a large flower garden to the present fashion,' wrote Robert Fish, a head gardener in the middle of the nineteenth century. The ingenuity needed to raise enough pelargoniums (or geraniums, as most of us call them) for parterres and borders as large as those at Eythrope has not diminished with the passing of time. A thousand pelargoniums are grown to fill the parterre and to furnish urns and pots around the house. These are planted out in mid-May and removed towards the end of September. In the early years, the parterre scheme was based on the scarlet 'Paul Crampel' and coral 'Crystal Palace Gem', which are old Victorian varieties. These are no longer grown for the parterre but are instead used to fill the beds at the front of the house. A softer scheme more recently chosen for summer in the parterre uses the variegated 'Grey Lady Plymouth' and another Victorian favourite, the silvery pink zonal 'Lady Ilchester', alongside the scented heliotrope 'Chatsworth'. For the entrance borders in the walled garden more pelargoniums are needed and here the cerise 'Vera Dillon' is combined with dark-leaved aeoniums and *Salvia involucrata* 'Boutin'. We tend to think of bedding schemes that include pelargoniums as municipal, but mixed with other tender plants, as they are at Eythrope, they become much more interesting. As well as all those grown for planting outside, there are the scented-leaf pelargoniums in pots, which form the summer display in the auricula theatre. For indoor decoration, geraniums are as useful as they were in Miss Alice's day but here the choice is not restricted to period varieties.

Cuttings are taken in the autumn, directly from plants growing outdoors. If they were lifted for stock plants it would take much longer to raise the plants that are needed. Where greenhouse space is more limited than it is at Eythrope this might be an option, but plants would then be much smaller the following spring. The geranium cuttings are grown seven to a 15-cm/6-inch clay pot and some will be ready to be potted on into 9-cm/3½-inch plastic pots before Christmas. Any older plants will be ready to move up into 12-cm/5-inch pots and the larger ones will be fed. All through January and February the work of moving plants on and pinching them out so that they grow into bushy specimens will happen in house number 5, where the temperature is kept at 10°C/50°F. The larger stock plants which will go into containers indoor are trimmed and sometimes staked. When they return from a spell in the house the dead leaves need picking off, and the task of 'cleaning over' appears regularly in the gardeners' diaries. Where so many plants are grown under cover hygiene is vital.

By March, some geraniums will be in 18-cm/7-inch pots to make particularly large specimens for the house; those to be planted outside will by that time be in 12-cm/5-inch pots. The work of potting on lasts until the start of May when the plants that are not being used for bedding

Opposite
'Paton's Unique' pelargoniums ready to be taken up to the house.

or to fill the auricula theatre for the summer display are moved into their summer quarters, where they fill the whole length of one house. During the summer any dead flowers or leaves are removed. Walking through the brightly coloured blooms, with that pungent mix of minty, lemony fragrances, is one of the best sensations of the year.

By the end of September it will be time to start the whole process again, taking cuttings that will fill the garden and decorate the house in the following year. This continues year on year.

Pelargoniums have always been a good standby for interior decoration – in cottages as well as in mansions. On sunny windowsills they will flower through the coldest months, and even the scented-leaf varieties that do not flower bring welcome greenery inside the house during the winter. *P. tomentosum*, which has handsome furry leaves, will survive in shade. The lemon-scented leaves of *P.* 'Mabel Grey' need a sunnier place. At Eythrope the pots of geraniums are used on tables in the rooms for two to three weeks. They then need a recovery period in the greenhouse before they can be used again.

Some of the favourite varieties grown for decoration indoors are 'Apple Blossom Rosebud', which dates from 1870, 'Fair Ellen', the oak-leaf geranium with almond-scented leaves, darkest red 'Lord Bute', 'Copthorne', a long-flowering scented-leaf variety with larger pinky-mauve flowers marked with purple, and the Regal pelargonium 'Carisbrooke', which has shell-pink blossoms feathered with purple. An unusual variety is the brilliant 'Ardens', which dates from 1820. It has lacquer-red tiny flowers, eight or more to a stem, with a darker streak down the middle, and is notoriously hard to propagate except from selected pieces of the tuber. It does also seem to need more water than most geraniums (except in winter, when it can be kept drier).

Clay pots with seven pelargonium cuttings each.

Potting on a well-rooted cutting.

Potting on a second time.

Stopping the plant.

Cuttings are covered with a sheet of polythene (which is turned twice daily) until they root.

PROPAGATION

One whole greenhouse 27 metres/90 feet long is dedicated to propagation. Here the plant factory line is kept moving all year with Jonathan in charge, helped by Naomi for flowers and Paul for vegetables. Seed sowing and pricking out are methodical tasks and watching the gardeners working so carefully and thoughtfully exercises a hypnotic effect. It is almost like the experience of seeing a potter throw a pot – you recognize that sense of purpose and confidence that only comes from long practice. First, the pots and trays to be used must be clean. The compost is John Innes no. 1 made with coir with a base fertilizer added, and this is spilled out of a sack (which keeps it moist) into the potting area. The seed trays are filled to overflowing. Once levelled with a piece of wood like a ruler, a layer of vermiculite is sprinkled on top and then the contents of the tray are tamped down with a wooden block that exactly fits the seed tray. The seed is sown as sparsely as possible. It is watered with about eleven passes of a can with a fine rose (upside down) and then left to germinate for a week without further watering. Once the seedlings emerge, watering is cautious. New seedlings are often drowned by inexperienced gardeners. The watering is never done with a hose but always from a watering can. The water is taken from a tap but cans are filled and left inside so that they are at the right temperature for the small plants. The tanks under the benches add moisture to the air, but are not used for watering

The sowing year starts towards the end of February, with the two plants that need cold temperatures (or stratification) to germinate. These are *Francoa ramosa* and *Persicaria orientale*, which are started off in the unheated glasshouse dedicated to the auriculas. Once they have germinated, they are moved to a section of the propagation house which is heated to 10°C/50°F. The quantities of seeds that require warmer temperatures – such as nicotianas, tithonias and especially the large-leaf basil – are sown at 15°C/60°F in the prop house. The lettuce-leaf basil from Suttons, which has become a speciality of the garden, is then sown at fortnightly intervals throughout the summer until the end of July. This will remain in pots, in the warm and humid section of the prop house known as the 'Basilry', after other plants have been moved out and hardened off.

The peak months in the prop house are February to April, for sowing and pricking out, and September and October, for taking cuttings. Pricking out is done once the plants have developed the second pair of leaves, which might be two to three weeks after sowing. The aim is to minimize root disturbance. Those plants that really dislike being repotted will be grown in plugs. These include some of the hardy biennials and annuals, particularly the umbelliferae, which tend to bolt from a spring sowing. *Ammi majus* and *Orlaya grandiflora* are candidates for plugs, as are poppies, nigella, linaria, silene and zinnias.

Seeds collected in the garden are dried and packed.

Compost is crumbled.

Compost is levelled with a piece of wood.

Evenly spaced holes are made for pricking out.

Some seedlings do better in plugs rather than trays.

Lettuce is grown from pelleted seed.

Broad beans need deep pots.

Leaf cuttings are shown at the back of the staging.

Opposite
Nicotianas and
antirrhinums waiting to
be potted individually.

Pages 140–141
Bright blue *Salvia patens*
and shocking-pink
S. microphylla 'Cerro
Potosi' with *Dahlia
australis*, all grown from
cuttings under glass.

Pages 142–143
As soon as the growing
season starts, the
propagation house is
filled with plants. Once
the weather warms up,
the nicotiana seedlings
in the foreground will
be hardened off to make
space for other plants.

Sometimes the gardeners trial seeds in plugs and trays at the same time to see if there is any advantage in one method over the other, so they are well aware of what method will suit each plant. All the seedlings grown in trays will be potted on into a general purpose coir compost in trays and, once established, on into 9-cm/3½-inch plastic pots. Those grown in plugs will go straight into pots. All of them will be hardened off gradually, by being moved into cooler conditions under glass, until they are finally ready to go outside. Any plant that has to be in a pot for more than a month will be fed with Maxicrop or Vitax liquid feed.

Pricking out from seed sown in trays is done so that there are twenty-four evenly spaced plants to a tray. First the tiny seedlings are gently eased out of their tray. (Heavy compost makes this difficult, so it does matter that the soil is friable and does not stick to the roots or make it hard to extract the plants.) With the blunt end of a wooden dibber, four holes are marked in a row along the top of the new tray. The first plant is then lifted into a hole and firmed in with the dibber, with as little handling as possible. 'Two movements are all you need,' Jonathan says, as he rapidly makes more holes and plants another two rows to the halfway mark and then continues in the same way with another dozen to fill the lower part of the tray. It looks deceptively easy, but turning out tray after tray of perfectly spaced plants that have been moved from cradle to kindergarten without a single mishap is skilled work.

The first cuttings to be taken in September are the heliotropes, which need to be done early. They are propagated twenty at a time to a half tray from soft-tip cuttings which are dipped in fresh rooting powder and then set into a 50/50 mix of coir compost and perlite and put to root on a bench in the warmest section of the greenhouse. There are ten varieties of heliotrope grown for bedding or pots, including four hundred plants of the particularly scented 'Chatsworth', destined for the parterre and for pots near the house The trays of cuttings are covered with a sheet of white polythene (which is turned twice a day), until they have rooted – which takes about a fortnight if conditions are right. Cuttings of salvias and other tender perennials will be taken in the same way, but not until October.

FERNS AND CLIVIAS

Although in most grand Victorian houses head gardeners arranged elaborate floral decorations for the dining room, in other rooms potted plants of an indestructible kind – such as aspidistras, palms and ferns – were mainly used. At Waddesdon anthuriums were also popular, and a whole glasshouse was devoted to the culture of these highly coloured tropical arums. Victorian rooms tended to be dark and draughty, and the fumes from gas lighting and heating produced an atmosphere that was unlikely to be suitable for many of the plants that are brought indoors to flower in pots today. When Mrs James took over the running of Waddesdon she wrote that the only major change to the way the rooms looked in Baron Ferdinand's day was the introduction of more flowers, rather than palms and evergreens. She did not mention ferns specifically, but it is likely that they as well as palms and the indefatigable aspidistra were used to decorate the Victorian Manor.

Ferns were hugely popular in the second half of the nineteenth century: their fronds appeared on everything from textiles to pottery to garden seats. Fern collecting was such a craze that Charles Kingsley pronounced that young ladies who engaged in pteridomania were 'more active, more cheerful, more self-forgetful over it, than they would have been over novels and gossip, crochet and Berlin-wool'. We do not know that Baron Ferdinand and his sister pursued fern collection, but we can only assume that they were not immune from the fashion of their time.

These days ferns are more popular outside than indoors. They are invaluable plants for shady places and carefully chosen can provide greenery throughout the cold winter months. At Eythrope they are used in an area where snowdrops and winter-flowering shrubs are grown. This corner of the garden is outside the scope of the present book, but it is worth noting that the hart's-tongue fern, *Asplenium scolopendrium*, and *Polystichum setiferum* 'Pulcherrimum Bevis' (Divisilobum Group) are both beauties that are easily grown in many gardens. They will thrive in shade and do not need particularly moist soil. They can even be grown in pots for winter effect. The strong shapes of ferns provide useful punctuation marks in flowery gardens and there are several forms which can cope with dry shade.

The Pavilion also has its share of fern decoration – along with many more cut flowers than would ever have been seen in Miss Alice's day – but often these are cut leaves of maidenhair used to provide backing for smaller vases. Ferns grown in 18-cm/7-inch plastic pots are also placed in large oval china footbaths and these will last indoors for several weeks, far longer than any vase of flowers.

The maidenhair fern *Adiantum venustum*, with its filigree leaves and black stems, is a beautiful plant from the Himalayas. Grown out of doors it is deciduous and will not survive hard winters. At Eythrope, the ferns are kept in greenhouse number 3, which is shaded but not heated

Opposite
Clivias thrive under the staging and will flower happily in the shade.

145

in summer and regularly damped down. The ferns are given a high-nitrogen feed once a week in summer, and in winter the temperature never falls below 10°C/50°F. Like geraniums, their leaves need regular cleaning over. They are propagated by division at a temperature of 10–12°C/50–54°F.

Clivias were introduced to England in 1815. They were named after Lady Charlotte Clive, Duchess of Northumberland, who was the first to grow them in Britain. They do not appear in gardening books until the end of the century, and they remained expensive plants for years, but their exotic looks would have been popular with the Victorians, who loved anything tropical. Collected from South Africa, where they grow in woodland, they are easy to grow in shady, frost-free conditions under glass. They are quite happy to live under the staging in the glasshouse at Eythrope, where they are watered once a week, never fed and only repotted about once every five years. Their striking glossy leaves and showy orange flowers are a welcome feature indoors in early spring. Clivias can be grown outdoors in warmer zones, but they do best left undisturbed in pots that are 20 cm/8 inches or larger, with the necks of the bulbs visible above the soil. They can be top-dressed rather than repotted. At Eythrope they are kept dry, cool and shaded in winter, from November until after Christmas, when watering is increased until they flower. After flowering, water decreases while they rest, until they start building up to flowering again. In summer they can live outside in a shady place, but at Eythrope, where there is room to keep them in the greenhouse, they spend all year under the staging.

BORDERS

FLOWER BORDERS

There are several borders in the walled garden. As you enter through the iron gates under the archway, double beds line the path leading to the raised pool, where stone toads spout at one another across a backdrop of greenhouses. These beds are seasonal, bedded out for spring with tulips or hyacinths and wallflowers and in summer with pelargoniums and aeoniums, so there is always something showy to see at the start of a garden tour. Bedding can be an expensive business, but not when all the plants are grown on site. Magenta-pink pelargoniums 'Vera Dillon', for instance, all come from a cutting of a plant admired at Chatsworth. Gardeners are generous, and everyone enjoys a plant with a history.

There is so much to take in on a first visit that instinctively your steps slow. Distracted, you might choose to turn towards the cherry house before reaching the pool. If you do, you find yourself on a path that runs between a more relaxed planting, where the mix is more permanent than bedding. The paired rose beds run across the axis to the main glasshouse range and this is a place to wander at midsummer on the way to pick some cherries. Here old-fashioned roses are beautifully trained on ironwork domes made locally and at their feet is a froth of flowers from June to September. The colours are soft pinks and purples, with lemon-yellow aquilegias. The roses are not long-flowering modern hybrids, but they have a second flush in September and when they are out the air is heavy with their scent. Visitors have been known to wander into the garden before breakfast and pick up a trug for a little deadheading. This task has always been a traditional pastime for the ladies of the house and it is an agreeable way of getting involved with the flowers, as the silky petals flutter into the basket.

If, instead, you choose to enter by the larger gate to the walled garden, your walk will take you past mixed borders planted for all-year interest. These are around the outside of the courtyard buildings, where some of the gardeners live and where flowers and produce are collected on the shelves outside Sue's office before being taken up to the house.

The route round the outside of the yard leads to a rondel of yew hedges, with paths leading out of it. Here you might turn into the kitchen garden via the fruit tunnel, or take the path to the right down the rose borders towards the cherry house, or – best of all – choose to walk down the wide grass path between the two herbaceous beds that are the great glory of this walled garden. They run up to a wire rose arbour that came from the Aviary at Waddesdon, whose twin is now in the garden at the Dairy. The ground rises to the arbour where there are benches to sit under beautifully trained China roses that would have been familiar to Miss Alice.

These borders only come into their own after midsummer. Autumn is the moment when sunlight slants low and gold down the huge plantings that have waited all summer for their moment to arrive. In a

Page 148
The herbaceous borders in late summer. The wire rose arbour was once in the Aviary at Waddesdon.

Opposite
The paired rose beds on the path to the cherry house. In the foreground is *Rosa* 'Baronne Prévost', trained on hazel benders.

large garden like this there are other places to turn for seasonal effects. The rose border is the focus of attention through June and July and although the herbaceous borders have a few early plants, the second half of the year is when they are designed to be at their best. These are real old-fashioned herbaceous beds – no shrubs, no bulbs and certainly no grasses. Although Sue Dickinson might in any other garden have been tempted to introduce a mixed border, Eythrope is different. These showpiece arrangements were always designed to be nearer in feeling to high Victorian borders than to modern schemes. This part of the garden looks like an old watercolour, or one of the early autochrome photographs of the Waddesdon gardens. At the end of the vista between the beds, the wirework rose arbour is another echo of the old Waddesdon garden that Miss Alice would have known.

Herbaceous borders were the latest thing in the middle of the nineteenth century. This may seem surprising, as people tend to think of Victorian gardens as filled with bright bedding in primary colours. But herbaceous borders were certainly a feature at the Manor as well as at Eythrope, and they would have had a gentler, less organized look, with softer colours, than what is now fashionable. More structure, less staking and a longer, brighter, flowering season is what gardeners now like. I know of very few borders entirely planted with hardy flowers – the mixed border which includes shrubs, bulbs, half-hardies and grasses is what most people prefer in the twenty-first century. Michael Calnan, Head of Gardens at the National Trust, admits that he finds it hard to think of any pure example of a Victorian-style herbaceous border in his care. The border in the private garden at Arley Hall in Cheshire was purely herbaceous when it was first designed, in 1840, but that now includes shrubs. At Westonbirt, two early Victorian herbaceous borders have been restored in the Italian Garden, but they are on a much smaller scale. The borders at Eythrope are rare examples of the style of this period.

On an autumn walk around the garden, with the peppery scent of phlox hanging in the air, you can enjoy the hazy, misty groups of Michaelmas daisies as they start to flower. All through October, as leaves begin to turn russet red and gold, wandering down the beds on the wide grass path is the purest of pleasures. You might even add the taste of some Muscat grapes or a bite of crisp apple as you walk. Who could not feel happy at the rarely united beauty of sight, scent and taste that this paradise provides? Sometimes the sound of a clucking hen carries from the orchard, adding another delight, and if the walker turns left beyond the rose arbour into the pot garden, there will be plenty of leaves to feel, with different textures and smells. Verbena (*Aloysia citrodora*), with its rough rasp of lemony leaves, will linger on your hands all day. Interested visitors may say, as gardeners often do, 'I'd love a bit of that aster, or the name of that particularly delicious apple,' and, in the generous spirit of the place, there are few people who leave empty-handed. Especially in autumn, when the gardens at Eythrope brim with their own abundant harvest festival.

HERBACEOUS BORDERS

The herbaceous borders are planted for late summer and autumn flowering. From May on, there is plenty of interest in the rose beds and in the bedded-out borders, but by September, when the big double beds are in full flower, the whole garden becomes a feast of colour and scent. This is the moment when Paradise really is filled with plenty.

In the nineteenth century herbaceous plants were arranged in smallish groups of each plant, with a large variety of different types. At Waddesdon the herbaceous borders, backed by yew hedges as the Eythrope ones are today, contained a medley of colours and plants which seemed very foreign to the young French gardener Marcel Gaucher, who spent three years at the Manor from 1922. He wrote of banked borders with the tallest plants at the back and smaller ones in the front, all set out like a jigsaw puzzle. Care with colour groupings and leaf textures are modern preoccupations that did not generally feature in these early perennial border plantings. At Waddesdon, lupins, delphiniums, heleniums and foxgloves were placed at the back, grading down through phlox, nepeta and penstemons to sedums and saxifrages at the front. All along the border, about 4 metres/12 feet apart, were iron frames with sweet peas growing through them. Sue admits that she did not try to emulate this. However, she did endeavour to ignore prevailing theories of plant associations when she planned the scheme, and the plants are arranged in billowy ribbons to create the effect of an old watercolour. Gertrude Jekyll chose a lozenge shape, rather than circles, for groups and at Eythrope that is also the prevailing style. The varieties of flowers popular in 1880 – asters, aconitum and phlox – dominate the Eythrope borders. (In the 1890s there were 144 asters listed in contemporary seed catalogues, as well as some intriguing double white phlox.) The old-fashioned planting makes the beds look very different from most schemes today, with colour harmonies rather than the strong clashes now in favour, and a charming gracefulness that has been lost to more modern schemes. The arrangement of the plants is, however, much more of our time than Miss Alice's. Heights are not banked from front to back, and the whole effect is a subtle blend rather than *bariolage*, the motley appearance which the young French gardener found so strange.

Earlier in the year, the double beds leading to the wirework rose arbour are filled with pleasing hummocks of green, but by July the phlox will have started to flower, releasing its sharp peppery scent as you pass. There will be a few penstemons out and these keep going as the border builds to its September climax. Some plants are attention-grabbers well before the flower buds begin to colour. *Aconitum carmichaelii* has a strong, statuesque form, and the green globes of echinops are shapely features before their thistle heads turn steely blue as the days shorten. There are several groups of white *Leucanthemella serotina* (syn. *Chrysanthemum uliginosum*) and airy *Galega* × *hartlandii*,

Opposite
Aster amellus 'Veilchenkönigin'. pale long-flowering *A.* × *frikartii* 'Mönch' and the crimson form of *Dahlia coccinea* mingle in the early autumn borders.

161

Opposite
Aster lateriflorus var.
horizontalis, *Aster*
amellus, *Penstemon*
'King George V',
Gaura lindheimeri and
Rudbeckia laciniata
'Herbstsonne' in
the borders.

and at the edges of the bed are cloudy *Nepeta govaniana* – the pale yellow catmint – gaura and the well-defined shapes of *Aster lateriflorus* 'Prince'. Then the great billows of Michaelmas daisies take over. These are mostly varieties of *A. novae-angliae*, which are more resistant to the mildew that can disfigure asters in dry years. The hazy mauves and pinks – with a flash of yellow from goldenrod – will keep going until the first frosts.

After a top dressing of the seaweed meal and Vitax that is used all over the garden, the main task in these beds is tactful staking. Although the plants are packed closely together there is always a danger that they will collapse, and they need to be securely staked well before that can happen. Ideally, staking should be started in the third week of May and at Eythrope peasticks are used. Gardeners with no peasticks can use canes and string as they do at Great Dixter, winding the string round each stem and anchoring the whole to a central bamboo; or they can practise the Chelsea Chop, reducing each plant by a third around the time of the Chelsea Flower Show at the end of May.

Plants need to be staked to within 15 cm/6 inches of their ultimate height so that when they flower no sticks can be seen. The peasticks circle the plants, with a few set among the stems. The aim is to prevent a gap in the centre of the clump. The stick must support the plant, so it needs to go into the ground firmly. Once in, the tops are bent over for the plant to grow through, or trimmed so that the flowering spikes rise above the peasticks.

Watering is another chore. Porous hose was laid throughout the beds for several years, in lines about 60 cm/2 feet apart, but this arrangement suffered from work in the borders (it is all too easy to put a fork through a hose). Watering is now done with an overhead sprinkler, in the evening.

Plants need to be divided regularly: at Eythrope about every three years is usual. Asters are better moved in the spring, but phlox can be split at the end of the flowering season

With any border that has a grass path next to it, maintenance of the edges can be difficult. At Eythrope there is a line of bricks laid flush with the grass. This allows plants to spill over in clumps and adds to the generous look of the place.

ROSES

By the middle of the nineteenth century roses were a craze among English gardeners. The Victorians loved the luxuriance, colour and fragrance of their flowers and since the introduction of the Chinese roses – around the time that Jane Austen was writing her novels – it was easy to have roses in flower for much longer than had been possible when limited to the European varieties.

Over three hundred roses were grown in Miss Alice's garden at Eythrope and the heavy clay soil still suits them well. Many of her tea roses were grown under glass in a special rose house and a few of these tender tea roses still flower on the back walls of the vinery. Most of the shrub roses in the borders that lead up to the cherry house, off the main axis to the greenhouses, were introduced before Miss Alice's years at the Pavilion. After the first flush of blooms at midsummer, all of them have a second flowering period in September. The types included are Portland roses, Bourbons and Hybrid Perpetuals. The Portlands belong to a group of hybrids developed from a rose grown in the Duchess of Portland's garden at the start of the nineteenth century. This variety flowers on and off every six weeks and will often provide a few roses at Christmas. All the Portlands smell wonderful. The pink 'Jacques Cartier' and the crimson 'De Resht' are good examples. Bourbons, which are a step closer to modern Hybrid Tea roses, are taller than the Portlands. The best performers at Eythrope are 'Madame Isaac Pereire' and the striped 'Honorine de Brabant'. Hybrid Perpetuals were a later progression in nineteenth-century rose breeding, bringing richer colours and longer flowering to the rose palette. 'Baronne Prévost' is one of the best of these.

Victorian rose beds might have had a little mignonette or a few violas growing under the bushes, but the Eythrope rose beds now have much more underplanting than Miss Alice would have recognized. A lemon-yellow long-spurred aquilegia is a feature well before the roses appear and later in the year there are pinks and blues from penstemons, salvias, cosmos and cleomes to keep the border in flower between the first and second flush of roses.

At Sissinghurst, where Vita Sackville-West was one of the first to return to the old-fashioned rose varieties, her gardeners, Pam Schwerdt and Sibylle Kreutzberger, developed a pruning system for shrub roses which contains their often ungainly habits and encourages the bushes to maximum flowering. This was a refinement of a technique which the two famous gardeners had been shown at Waterperry. It is this system, which Sue learnt when she worked at Sissinghurst, that has been adopted at Eythrope.

For the taller roses, ironwork lattice domes were made by the local blacksmith, who also made the pear tunnel. Placed at the back of the border, these stay in place all year. The roses are pruned and trained around mid-February. All weak shoots are first cut out and strong

165

Opposite
Training rose 'Gros
Choux de Hollande'
on an iron frame
(with more work
still to be done).

branches are tipped and pulled as far down as possible to almost horizontal and then tied on to the iron frame. The point of this is to prevent apical dominance (the tendency that all plants have to flower at the top at the expense of the side shoots). Once the shoots have been lowered, it is extraordinary to see how fast and how vigorously buds appear evenly all along the main side stems and on these secondary growths roses will burst in June. The spacing between the main side shoots varies a little, but ideally is about 45 cm/18 inches (although at Eythrope this is done by eye).

The lower roses at the front of the bed are pruned and tied in a little later and, for these, 6-foot/1.8-metre hazel benders (from the woods) are used. Three poles are allotted to each individual bush: they are bent into an arch around the bush to provide the support needed for the summer. The hazel arch must be firmly anchored in the ground so that the side shoots of each rose can be tied to the arches like a great spider. Pruning principles are the same as on the iron wigwams, but instead of being trained to curve round a frame, the rose shoots are fanned out to reach the hazel arches that surround them, with subsequent shoots tied to the first branches in all directions to make a pleasing dome shape. Sue stresses the importance of avoiding gaps and making sure the centre is open. The finished bush makes a glorious mound which will be covered with roses at midsummer. The structure of the pruning is beautiful before the roses come into leaf.

Hard pruning and training will get the best from roses, but they do need feeding to encourage them back into growth. Leafmould, seaweed meal and Vitax Q4 are all added to the beds in spring. Most old roses are martyrs to blackspot but this is rarely a problem at Eythrope. This may be because when the roses are pruned every single growing tip is removed (blackspot overwinters as dormant spores in the growing tips of rose bushes).

The rose stems are tied to hoops of hazel.

Working from boards prevents compaction of winter soil.

Hazel benders are pushed into the ground to make a hoop shape.

The rose stems are tied down to the hoops.

The finished shape is neat and elegant.

BEDDING OUT

We know that Miss Alice was responsible for the colourful mounded planting in the parterre at Waddesdon and, from contemporary photographs of both Waddesdon and Eythrope, that much of the bedding was as exotic as the fashion of the day. But her letters to her head gardener, Johnson, contain more about fruit and vegetables than they do about flowers. A useful account of a visit to Eythrope by a writer for the *Bucks Herald* in 1890 is more revealing and suggests that she may have been a horticultural innovator. The writer's description of a giant wirework bird studded with lobelias and trailing greenery (see page 19) long predates the *Gardeners' Chronicle* article of 1899 of a visit to Halton, another neighbouring Rothschild house, where 'a series of extraordinary beds had extended carpet bedding into a vertical dimension: a cushion bed planted to represent a huge ottoman with cords and tassels, two large vases covered with succulents and other plants, just as a Dresden China vase may sometimes be seen studded with shells.' This is quoted by Brent Elliott in his definitive work on the Victorian garden as 'a new development in carpet bedding', but it could perhaps have been an exercise in keeping up with Miss Alice.

All nineteenth- and early twentieth-century gardens leaned heavily on bedding out to provide colour all year. It is a style that has almost entirely faded from private gardens these days, but at Eythrope it is still practised in several areas, with an interesting modern twist. The miniature parterre near the house, where Miss Alice once had flower beds in a style that was more naturalistic than the geometric style she chose for her Italian garden, has been replaced with beds again. (The design was taken from a simple layout shown in Shirley Hibberd's 1871 *The Amateur's Flower Garden.*) Today it is filled with geraniums and heliotropes. Both plants were popular in Victorian parterres. The current scheme uses old varieties which Miss Alice could have known and grown, although combining salmon-pink 'Vesuvius' with dark crimson and pale pink pelargoniums – as described in the *Bucks Herald* account of the Italian garden – seems strident today. The modern scheme has the pale pink flowers of *Pelargonium* 'Lady Ilchester' among the silvery leaves of *P.* 'Grey Lady Plymouth', with *Heliotropium* 'Chatsworth' planted throughout the beds for scent. An earlier scheme for the parterre included two other geraniums which would have been familiar to Miss Alice. These are the scarlet 'Paul Crampel' and 'Crystal Palace Gem', with gold-variegated foliage (records confirm that she definitely grew the latter). These are now grown near the front door, with more heliotropes and the yellow *Abutilon* 'Canary Bird' as a dot plant. In spring tulips and wallflowers fill all the beds near the house and varieties of these often change. Recently, badgers have become a nuisance, so hyacinths in several colours are being trialled for spring bedding instead of tulips.

Opposite
Tulips 'Avignon', 'Dordogne' and 'Menton', planted out in the vinery border, glow in shot-silk sunset pinks and oranges.

171

In the walled garden, the entrance borders are designed to look exotic – what Sue describes as 'over the top Victorian'. Succulents were often a feature of Victorian bedding and here the dark-leaved *Aeonium* 'Zwartkop' is used among dahlias 'Arabian Night', with shocking pink *Salvia involucrata* 'Boutin'. This form of *S. involucrata* has an Award of Garden Merit from the RHS. It is not as tall as 'Bethellii', but flowers a fortnight earlier and is a little hardier. More showy colour comes from *Pelargonium* 'Vera Dillon', whose magenta flowers have a scarlet flash, and *Canna × ehemanii*, with green leaves and soft crimson blooms, also adds an exotic touch.

Under the pear tunnel is a much softer bedding scheme, where pale blue *Salvia patens* 'Cambridge Blue' dominates. This can be grown from saved tubers in 12-cm/5-inch pots, but at Eythrope the preferred method is to raise new plants from seed sown in early March and then planted out from 9-cm/3½-inch pots. Mixed with the salvias are the filigree leaves of *Argyranthemum gracile* 'Chelsea Girl' and above both of these is a tracery of stems and pincushion purple flowers of *Verbena bonariensis*, which are grown annually from soft tip cuttings. Although the beds are in dappled shade from the arched pears the flowers do not seem to suffer. The spring scheme is less easy to arrange. For years there were tulips here in a range of mixed colours, like old-fashioned boiled sweets, but pheasants repeatedly dug them out. A barricade of hazel twigs was partly effective in protecting the bulbs, but it was time-consuming to arrange the defences. Recently a change to something easier has been tried; the latest look is for mixed polyanthus in older varieties which do not have the large eye of the hybrids now offered by most garden centres.

The bed in front of the vine house has a mixture of oval-shaped tulips in different pinks, raised in France in the 1990s. 'Menton', 'Avignon' and 'Dordogne' are large late-flowering beauties. They are laid out one variety at a time in order to get the shot-silk look of broken sunset colours which makes this bed so eye-catching.

In summer the vine bed is occupied by the many different varieties of salvia that are an Eythrope special. This hazy arrangement of flowers is modern rather than Victorian, but the gardens of Miss Alice, both in England and in Grasse, were always famous for their botanical interest and innovation, combined with artistic grouping.

Opposite
The parterre in summer, with *Heliotropium* 'Chatsworth', *Pelargonium* 'Lady Ilchester' and *P.* 'Grey Lady Plymouth'.

When bulbs – here tulips – are planted out, string lines ensure accuracy.

Flame-coloured tulip 'Dordogne' goes in first.

Coral 'Menton' is added in the gaps.

The bulbs are planted from the path or from boards.

Box plants originally surrounded the parterre, but when box disease struck they were replaced by *Ilex crenata*. These plants never flourished, and the decision was made to try box again. Here *Buxus sempervirens* is shown being planted. An effective cure for the virus has recently become available. Also, *B. sempervirens* has always seemed to be less susceptible to disease than the dwarf form, *B.s.* 'Suffruticosa'.

WINTER

The mixed border which wraps round the outside of the courtyard buildings is planted for all-year interest. Under the pinnacle tower is a corkscrew hazel, *Corylus avellana* 'Contorta' (commonly known as 'Harry Lauder's walking stick'), and the bed is punctuated by the bold bushes of golden yew, echoing the golden hedge that lines the main path to the garden. This particularly slow-growing form, *Taxus baccata* 'Elegantissima', is a feature of the gardens at Waddesdon and dates from the time of Baron Ferdinand and Miss Alice. It makes a dense hedge of more upright growth than ordinary yew. Any yew hedge that has outgrown its position can be regenerated by pruning back to the main trunk in April, followed by watering and feeding. And this hedge responded well to a hard cut-back on one side several years ago (although it did take three years to regrow).

Bushes of the repeat-flowering modern shrub rose 'Sally Holmes' are placed at intervals through the beds. The white single flowers are faintly scented, and their gold stamens echo the gold of the yew. This is an easy, disease-free rose, a strong grower that does not mind a bit of shade or a dry position and is rarely without a flower. More summer interest comes from the Hybrid Musk roses 'Buff Beauty', 'Prosperity', 'Cornelia', 'Penelope' and 'Danaë'.

Although there is plenty to see at other times of year, these beds are at their most impressive in winter, when the green background of shrubs comes into its own. Most of the shrubs grown are also invaluable for decoration indoors, at a time when cut flowers are scarce. As well as the corkscrew hazel there is also a large scented *Chimonanthus fragrans* which, because it needs to have old branches cut out to encourage new growth, will provide wonderfully fragrant stems indoors through January and February. The winter honeysuckle, *Lonicera fragrantissima*, is another candidate for hard pruning, which is useful for its yield of tiny flowers with a powerful honey smell. (One stem will scent a room indoors, but the flowers are so insignificant you wonder where the scent is coming from.) Ideally pruning should be done no later than May, so the winter harvest for vases indoors makes sense, because the flowers for the following year will appear on the new summer growth. *Viburnum × bodnantense* 'Charles Lamont' and *V. farreri* are equally obliging and responsive to pruning in the early part of the year.

Other scented shrubs that are picked for indoor use in the cold months are the invaluable evergreen Christmas box – the sarcococcas. Both *S. confusa* and *S. hookeriana* var. *digyna* are grown at Eythrope. Like the rest of the winter-flowering bushes here, sarcococca can stand any amount of pruning; and its scraps of white blossoms from Christmas until early February will fill vases indoors and make rooms smell like summer. Another sweetly scented shrub is *Abeliophyllum distichum*.

Opposite
The corkscrew hazel (*Corylus avellana* 'Contorta') under the pinnacle tower.

This is sometimes known as the white forsythia, but it is out much earlier than forsythia and the small flowers make it another useful variety to pick and bring indoors. Under all these winter-flowering shrubs there are in earliest spring plenty of hellebores. These are mainly the dark-petalled Galaxy strain developed by Jim Archibald, the plantsman whose nursery in Dorset was famous in the 1960s and 1970s. There are sheets of snowdrops carpeting the bed. One of the most remarkable facts about snowdrops is how quickly they increase with regular division. 'Lady Elphinstone' and 'Ophelia' are doubles which stand out well from a distance, as does the distinctive 'Magnet', with its drooping pedicel, and all of these have been increased over the years from a small stock of original bulbs.

SPECIAL
COLLECTIONS

FLORISTRY

At the Villa Victoria garden in Grasse, the flowers, from all over the world, that Miss Alice grew never failed to impress botanically minded visitors. We know that the Eythrope of her day included Dutch, Italian and Mexican gardens furnished with appropriate plants. There were cacti and exotics and masses of roses. So her plant collections must have been admired as much in England as on the French Riviera. Today the Paradise garden has some equally impressive plant collections, not in segregated areas of the main garden, as they would have been at the end of the nineteenth century, but in seasonal concentrations which add to the interest of a garden visit.

Quantities of carnations were grown under glass in Victorian times. In December 1880 William Taylor, the head gardener at Longleat, was able to cut a hundred carnations a day for buttonholes and bouquets. Miss Alice, who kept up with gardening trends, had over a thousand carnations under glass at Eythrope, and they were probably just as productive. In addition to a house for carnations, there was also a separate house for a thousand Malmaisons. These carnations originated in France as a chance seedling from the tree carnations which were popular winter flowers in the mid-nineteenth century. Because the new flower, which smelled of cloves, looked more like a rose than a carnation, it was named 'Souvenir de la Malmaison', after the rose commemorating the Empress Josephine's garden. These flamboyant belle époque flowers often decorated Oscar Wilde's buttonhole. (Although his were dyed a decadent green, rather than left to bloom in their natural shades of pink and white.) Malmaisons are still cultivated at Eythrope for summer flowering. The collection of outdoor dianthus is another garden speciality. But there are no longer any perpetual carnations that are forced in the winter months, as they would have been in their Victorian heyday.

Auriculas were probably not grown at Eythrope in Miss Alice's day but later a small collection of these decorative flowers was presented to the garden by a generous grower. They were so well liked that they became an annual spring feature and, as the collection grew, an auricula theatre in a suitably Frenchified style was designed to go in the corner of the walled garden. Clay pots (10 cm/4 inch) were bought for them from Whichford Pottery, so that they could be perfectly displayed, and a tiered circular glass stand which holds seventy plants at a time was found, so that plants could be brought indoors to be admired at close quarters.

Three other groups of plants have become important features in the modern garden. These are nerines, salvias and snowdrops.

In the first quarter of the twentieth century a collection of nerines was started at Exbury, another Rothschild house, by Lionel de Rothschild. After his death the collection went to Sir Peter Smithers, who selected many new forms and then returned the collection to Nicholas de Rothschild, the grandson of Lionel.

Page 180
Auriculas displayed on their tiered glass stand indoors.

Opposite
Salvia leucantha 'Purple Velvet' with *Dahlia* 'Magenta Star' in front of the vinery.

Opposite
White nerine 'Virgo',
with pink nerines, in
the glasshouse.

Pages 186 & 191
The May display in the
auricula theatre.

Page 187
Alpine auricula 'Argus'.

Pages 188–189
A close-up of the
auricula theatre display.

Page 190
Show Fancy auricula
'Green Lane'.

As sunny days become numbered, nerines are a tonic. The shocking-pink *Nerine bowdenii* may be familiar, as it grows outside in warm places, but *N. sarniensis* is even classier and more varied in colour and form. This is the type that is grown at Exbury. *N. sarniensis*, related to amaryllis, are sometimes referred to as jewel or diamond lilies, because their petals sparkle – exactly what is most needed in the dreariest months of the year. Early growers described this phenomenon as gold, or silver, dusting. Some varieties have wavy petals, which intensify the effect of refracted light. Shades of shocking pink or scarlet ribbon petals fill one section of a greenhouse at Eythrope in October and November. Out of doors, at the back of the bed where the dianthus are grown for cutting, are the hardier *bowdenii* types. The nerines provide a succession of dazzling flowers indoors from the beginning of October until about the middle of November.

Salvias are particular favourites in the Eythrope garden and a great variety of these late summer half-hardy perennials have been collected in recent years. There are over a thousand salvias in cultivation today and the number grows each year as more varieties are either found on plant hunting trips or hybridized. Of course Miss Alice would have been familiar with *Salvia splendens*, which grows wild in Brazil and has been in cultivation since 1822. This blazing scarlet salvia, which is almost as popular in modern bedding schemes as it was in her day, is often included in the parterre at Waddesdon and is grown in the salvia border at Eythrope. But there are newer, subtler salvias which have the same long-flowering qualities as *S. splendens*, with plenty of true blues among them. At Eythrope some salvias are grown in the pot garden; others are used to lengthen the season in the rose beds and many of them are collected in the vine house border for the summer. Every year there will be a different arresting form to catch the eye. *S.* 'Amistad', a deep and showy purple, which has only become available in the last couple of years, was introduced early at Eythrope.

Snowdrops are included as another botanical collection. Long before galanthomania caught on, Sue Dickinson was enjoying collecting this now fashionable genus. Many of the snowdrops are grown outside the Paradise garden (a large number in the huge winter garden, which is beyond the scope of this book), but there are some in the courtyard borders, and snowdrops are valuable for cutting in the winter months. It is fascinating to see how any plant-lover can always find room for their favourites.

AURICULAS

Auriculas were never High Victorian favourites in country houses. In 1822 Loudon wrote, 'The auricula is like the tulip, pink, etc., and a fine blow is rarely seen in the gardens of the nobility and gentry.' They were regarded as the flowers of labouring men, because they were so popular with home-working weavers throughout the seventeenth and eighteenth centuries. The constant care of their plants must have provided a welcome break from the loom; and the breeding and showing of these painted primulas also gave the weavers an elaborate social life at shows and dinners for like-minded fanciers.

However, though auriculas may not have been cultivated much by the upper classes in Miss Alice's day, they became very popular with a wide range of people from the twentieth century onwards. Artists enjoy their strange colour schemes, designers admire their period style – what Sacheverell Sitwell referred to as 'all the tidy brightness of the Regency'. Gardeners revel in both.

These decorative flowers are now a particular feature of the Eythrope spring. Every auricula grower will have variations on recipes for compost and on timings for potting, but the Eythrope routine certainly delivers results. Every April, two hundred well-grown plants in terracotta pots furnish the auricula theatre in the corner of the walled garden and another seventy will go indoors to be staged on a plant stand which allows close inspection of the different varieties. Auriculas still need the constant care that the home workers gave them. Careless handling or watering can disturb the mealy farina which silvers their grey-green leaves. Vine weevils can devour them, sun in summer will scorch them and rain in winter will drown them. The Eythrope plants spend most of the year in a cold and airy shaded greenhouse near the entrance to the garden, only leaving it when the flowers are out, to be displayed in the theatre, or for decoration in the house. (A cold frame makes a good alternative to an alpine house.)

The auricula year starts in February. Cuttings taken from plants in July of the previous year are moved from 7.5-cm/3-inch plastic pots to 9-cm/3½-inch clay pots. The compost used is the coir-based John Innes no. 2. (Some growers add a top dressing of grit, but this is not done at Eythrope.) This routine might take three weeks to accomplish.

When the established plants show signs of stirring, again usually in February, they will be given a weak nitrogen feed. (The newly potted cuttings will not be fed at this stage.) From March onwards, the older plants are given high-potash liquid fertilizer weekly. Dead leaves are removed and in April they are moved to the theatre. The display is changed three or four times a season and each show usually lasts for a month. As later plants come into flower the ones that are fading are returned to the glasshouse and their flowers are removed. All the flower stems are staked with kebab sticks and tied to these with raffia. Invisibly.

Opposite
A collection of Alpine
auriculas with gold
centres and one Show
Fancy grey with farina
on its leaves.

Auriculas do better when divided and repotted every year. Mature plants never perform well: three years from baby offset or cutting is about their limit. The moment for repotting at Eythrope is in July, when all the plants are reduced to one rosette and repotted in 9-cm/3½-inch pots in the usual compost with a little added bark. 10-cm/4-inch pans for more than one rosette were tried for a while, but the garden has now reverted to the single rosette in a smaller pot. The tip of the carrot-like root, which lengthens with age, is snipped off. Vine weevil can be a great nuisance to auriculas but the risk of these pests is lessened if all the old soil is removed. If a dose of a thiacloprid pesticide does have to be administered, then that is done after plants have settled into their new quarters, which will probably take about a month. Any offsets are potted into the 7.5-cm/3-inch plastic pots: these will make good plants for display in two years' time. After the annual operation of repotting is over, all the pots are put back in the glasshouse. They are arranged so that they are touching one another – this helps to keep the roots cool and to stop roots drying out. The plants are kept watered and are regularly picked over for dead leaves. They put on a little growth in September and this is often the moment to give them a boost of liquid fertilizer, but flowering is discouraged.

Some favourite varieties are the red Alpines 'Argus' and 'Prince John', which are easier to grow than darkest red 'Neat and Tidy'. Grey-green 'Prague' and sulphur-yellow 'Tomboy' are both Show Fancy auriculas with mealy silver leaves. These two are the pickiest and, in my opinion, the most beautiful of all. But with over a hundred varieties in the collection, including doubles and striped, an onlooker would find it hard to choose the best.

A division with a small root will grow better than one from an old tap root.

Auriculas in the glasshouse in summer.

Taking cuttings starts in July and goes on into the winter months.

Kebab sticks are used for staking.

Plants are tied to their stakes with raffia.

SALVIAS

In the latter half of the nineteenth century, salvias were popular as bedding plants with gardeners in search of ever more vivid and long-lasting colour. The South American scarlet sages *Salvia fulgens* and *S. splendens* and the bright blue *S. patens* added the brash brilliance, the ultimate zing, that everyone wanted in bedding schemes. They were certainly in use at Waddesdon, though perhaps not at Eythrope.

Salvias are still among the best plants to use for a long season of summer colour, but in an age when an airier, more natural look is fashionable it is the subtler shades and smaller flowers of the hardier meadow sages (derived from *S. nemorosa*) that tend to be chosen. However, the Eythrope collection of over fifty types of salvia is based the half-hardy perennial varieties popular with the Victorians.

Many salvia species and cultivars are trialled in the border in front of the vine house. They are also planted in the rose borders leading up to the cherry house, so that there is colour there while the roses rest. All of the salvias are treated as tender perennials, although several of the most glamorous varieties are borderline hardy. *S.* 'Indigo Spires', which is a deep purple blue, and the tall sky-blue *S. guaranitica* 'Blue Enigma' will stand the winter in well-drained soil (though, like all salvias, they need to be protected from slugs). The showy shocking-pink *S. involucrata* 'Bethellii' can also survive outdoors, but tends to flower so late when it does that it is often wiser not to try. Sue grows other *involucrata* cultivars and likes 'Boutin', which is not as tall as 'Bethellii', and 'Joan', which flowers for longer. The newer *S.* 'Amistad', with large blue-black flowers and shining foliage, is reported to be hardy, but it is too beautiful to lose so it is worth taking cuttings.

Cuttings of the salvia collection are taken in late September or early October. Those that are needed to add colour to the rose border will be taken mainly from the *leucantha* and *involucrata* types. The *leucantha* salvias have an intriguing downy look and their purple calyxes produce flowers that can be pink or white or deepest purple. *S.* 'Mulberry Jam' is a smaller *involucrata* hybrid, with darker flowers than 'Bethellii' or 'Boutin' or 'Joan', and plenty of these are grown among the roses.

In the vinery border each year there will be a great mix of newer varieties. Massed salvias can look too hazy on their own, so dark-leaved dahlias are included in this bed, as well as *Canna indica*, the parent of the modern hybrids. All the salvias are propagated from non-flowering shoots collected in a plastic bag, one variety at a time. The base of the cutting is taken below the node and varieties with large leaves have their leaves cut in half, which both reduces transpiration and makes for a neater cutting that takes up less room in the tray. The cuttings are dipped in rooting powder and then inserted twenty-four at a time into a half-tray. Once watered in, they are left on the bench, covered with white polythene which is turned twice a day for a fortnight, until they have rooted.

Opposite
Salvia concolor and *S. confertiflora* in the border in front of the vine house.

Page 200
The vinery border, with *Dahlia* 'Magenta Star', *Salvia leucantha* 'Purple Velvet', *S.* 'Amistad', *S. microphylla* 'Belize', *S. curviflora*, *S.* 'Trelawney' and *S. darcyi*.

Page 201
S. curviflora and *S.* × *jamensis* 'Red Velvet' in the vinery border, with the pit houses beyond.

Pages 202–203
The salvia border, with *S. darcyi*, *S.* × *jamensis* 'Señorita Leah', *Verbena rigida* f. *lilacina*, *Dahlia* 'Soulman' and *S.* 'Trelawney'.

NERINES

Nerines, which are invaluable for cut flowers in October and November, have become the nucleus of a new collection at Eythrope. The hardier *bowdenii* types, which are summer-leafing bulbs from areas of South Africa where rain falls in summer, are grown in the cut-flower borders, under the wall of the greenhouse. The *sarniensis* nerines, which also come from South Africa, are natives of wet winters and dry summers and are not frost-hardy, so they need to be grown under glass.

Nerine bowdenii can survive -15°C (5°F) outdoors. They need good drainage and in a dry summer will need watering to initiate flowering. At Eythrope they are grown in an east-facing border along the side of the first of the pit greenhouses. The very large 'Zeal Giant' is a hybrid of *N. bowdenii* and *N. sarniensis* that is surprisingly hardy and grows well outside at Eythrope. Other outdoor *bowdenii* cultivars that Sue rates highly are 'Mark Fenwick', 'Stefanie', 'Ostara' and 'Marjorie'. Some of the *bowdenii* crosses have proved less hardy. At Eythrope they are planted next to the wall of the greenhouse, so they are close to the heating pipes that run down the wall on the other side. In colder gardens, they may need to be overwintered indoors. In summer all *bowdenii* types should be outside in shade. Very hot temperatures under glass do not suit them.

Nerine sarniensis, often referred to as jewel – or diamond – lilies because of the way the petals glitter in the light, live inside all year. They need warmth but must not dry out completely or the bulbs shrivel, so they are damped over about once a month. From October they are kept at a temperature of 5°C/40°F in greenhouse number 4, but they spend the summer in the auricula house, which is cooler and well shaded. All nerines in pots are shy to flower if they do not get the conditions they need, and as buds are initiated as far ahead as two years before the flowers appear, they need conscientious care. The ideal for achieving the best flowers is good light and a summer temperature of 24°–27°C/ 75°–80°F in the dormant period. Once the buds nose through in the pots, which is usually about the end of August, watering starts, in imitation of the autumn rains which the *sarniensis* expect in their native habitat. They do not like too much water, and good drainage is important. When the flowers are finished the leaves will develop and from the time leafing begins the plants are fed with a high-potash fertilizer until the leaves die down. After this watering reverts to a monthly routine.

Nerines grown in pots like to be crowded and the compost needs to be one that drains well. At Eythrope they are grown in clay pots and only repotted when flowering falls off. The necks of the bulbs are planted above the soil level and the pots are top-dressed with grit. After repotting flowering may be less good. Mealy bug can be a problem. Thiacloprid prevents this and should be applied in the growing season.

Opposite
The necks of nerine bulbs need to stand proud of the pots, to keep them well drained.

Pages 206–207
Nerine 'Pink Triumph' in the glasshouse.

SNOWDROPS

Miss Alice spent her winters in the South of France and would rarely have enjoyed the snowdrops that were gaining popularity with English gardeners by the end of the nineteenth century. Canon Ellacombe, who wrote articles for *The Garden* about his garden on the edge of Bristol, described his love of these earliest bulbs. He grew numbers of the common snowdrop as well as examples of most of the species 'and would grow all if I could but some will not grow here. The Crimean snowdrop does very well and I like it for the pleasant story which tells what a delight it was to our soldiers when they saw it during the first dreadful winter of the Crimean war.' This is the wide-leaved *Galanthus plicatus*, which soldiers carried home with them from the Black Sea. The bulbs they brought back have been the forerunners of many coveted modern varieties, such as 'Diggory', 'Colossus' and 'Warham'. Crosses with the ordinary British native snowdrop *G. nivalis* have resulted in the beautiful and scented *G.* 'S. Arnott' and the Greatorex doubles. All of these are now grown at Eythrope, either in woodland areas or tucked into the beds around the courtyard.

There are more than seventy varieties of snowdrop grown at Eythrope. This may not be as many as can be found in the collections of some obsessive galanthophiles, but there are quite enough to detain other collectors. Among particular favourites is the very early *G. elwesii* 'Mrs Macnamara', which is always out in the first days of the New Year. This is a large snowdrop and there will be enough flowers to pick for a succession of several turns in a glass bowl indoors. Other early types are the Greatorex double 'Ophelia', which stands out well from a distance in drifts under the shrubs in the courtyard border and 'Limetree', which also makes a good spread. Also popular are *G. plicatus* 'Augustus', a chubby-leaved beauty which naturalizes well in grass, 'Hill Poë', a showy late double, 'Jacquenetta', an even fuller double from the Greatorex strain, and the simple 'Merlin', with inner segments of the petals in mysterious green.

Regular division has helped to increase all the snowdrops. This is time-consuming work which at Eythrope is done at the end of March and the start of April. Opinion is divided on when to lift and split *Galanthus*, and some experts think that June is a better time than just after flowering. But time is short in summer and provided the operation is done quickly, as it is at Eythrope, no harm should result.

Splitting snowdrops is important from both a practical and an aesthetic point of view. Large clumps dry out in the middle, which results in smaller non-flowering bulbs; and, moreover, congested bulbs can be prone to virus, so dividing them may help to avert trouble. Aesthetically, increasing the impact of drifts in the places where they grow is crucial. Eythrope, like Waddesdon, is a garden where scale and show always matter.

Opposite
Galanthus plicatus
'Augustus' naturalizes well, but as it can be prone to virus infection it is a good idea to keep it away from other snowdrops.

Pages 210–211
G. 'Limetree' is a variant of the early-flowering *G.* 'Atkinsii' (it was found flowering under a lime tree).

POTS
AND
TOPIARY

POTTED PLANTS AND
TAILORED TREES

Influenced by Italian gardens, the Victorians scattered urns and vases as exclamation marks around parterres or on terraces. These containers were usually planted with geraniums, particularly scarlet ones, perhaps with a tropical plant of architectural form at the centre of the vase. As trim and tidy as a Victorian posy with its concentric rings of flowers, they were a far cry from the modern fashion for groups of pots each holding a composition of different plants, which are allowed to sprawl and tumble exuberantly down the sides.

Container gardening is a contemporary way of gardening that especially suits the owners of small gardens (which includes most town-dwellers). The way we garden today has been far more influenced by Mediterranean clusters of pots outside doors than by formal Italian layouts. But although potscapes would have been unfamiliar to Miss Alice, the botanical interest and artful arrangements in the Eythrope pots might have earned her approval.

The Eythrope style is an inspiration to any gardener. Sue has a knack of combining plants in great cornucopias of colour, but there are also plenty of containers where the planting is restricted to one genus in each pot. Pots are used throughout the garden to draw the visitor through doors or gates. In some places, large pots add height and drama to an area, or create a sense of enclosure. Used imaginatively, pots can be a way of extending a border, so that the garden reaches out to envelop the onlooker. In all the pots, the planting schemes vary from year to year, although old favourites are often repeated.

There are horticultural treasures to be found in the pot garden in a corner of this modern version of Paradise. Under the south-facing wall, where the peach case used to be, is an enclosed space, a triangle of gravel, which is kept for special plants grown in terracotta pots. This is a collection arranged to display a variety of unusual flowers concentrated in one area. The plants vary from year to year but all of them are tender perennials or half-hardy shrubs which have been raised under glass.

Several different kinds of containers are used for growing plants. There is a hierarchy of stone near the house (as well as large terracotta pots). On the parterre terrace are some stone urns which are a legacy of Miss Alice's day, and these are still planted in a style which the original chatelaine would have recognized. A cordyline at the centre is surrounded by the ivy-leaf variegated *Pelargonium* 'Hederinum Variegatum' (syn. 'Duke of Edinburgh'), a geranium which flowers non-stop. Its sharp pink flowers and silvery leaves always look elegant even in rainy seasons. In the courtyard on the way to the kitchen garden the containers are the wooden tubs traditional in domestic and stable courtyards. In most other areas, terracotta pots are the preferred

Page 212
Tulips in the pot garden in spring. The red tulip in the foreground is 'Bastogne Parrot'.

Opposite
Heliotropium arborescens 'Princess Marina' and *Pelargonium* 'Yale' under *Abutilon* 'Nabob' in the corner of the walled garden devoted to plants in pots.

215

Opposite
Abutilon 'Canary Bird'.

Pages 218 & 223
The repetition of
Pelargonium 'Hederinum
Variegatum' gives unity
to the planting scheme.

Pages 219 & 222
P. 'Hederinum
Variegatum'.

Pages 220–221
White plumbago and
scented *Heliotropium
arborescens* 'Chatsworth'
near the Pavilion.

containers. All of these come from the Whichford Pottery and were designed by Jim Keeling. They are a strong red that goes well with the red ridge tiles on the roof of the courtyard buildings, which also top the garden walls. The tiles were added, to give the garden more unity, as part of the new design made when the present Lord Rothschild inherited Eythrope.

Terracotta pots have various advantages over plastic ones. They are heavy and will not blow over. They offer a little protection from extremes of weather and, as long as they can be raised off the ground in winter so that water can drain away, they are frostproof. Clay pots will always dry out faster than plastic, because the clay acts as a wick and draws moisture away from the earth to the air outside. (This can be helpful for those who are inclined to overwater.) On the other hand, being porous, terracotta pots will also absorb moisture from wet ground. Grouped together, the potted colonies create their own microclimate and do not dry out so quickly in hot weather. During very hot spells smaller pots can be stood on saucers with a bit of water in the bottom, but the saucers must be removed once the rain returns, so that pots never get waterlogged.

At Eythrope, the largest pots are 60 cm/2 feet in diameter. For displays outside nothing smaller than 18 cm/7 inches is used, as small pots can dry out too quickly. The shapes are varied, and there are many plain flower pots in different sizes, as well as some half pots, for a variety in height that adds interest to the display.

Another corner of the walled garden is filled with topiary – tailored shapes in box, yew and *Lonicera nitida*, and wire frames on which ivy is trained. The topiary garden at Eythrope is an interesting example of an organically realized and collaborative design. Originally this space was planned as a lawn with mulberry trees. The topiary scheme began with a couple of wire frames of horses (racing has always been a Rothschild passion) placed on this small lawn. Ivy was trained on the frames, but Lord Rothschild thought the horses looked too isolated. So Sue devised a topiary world inspired by Nathaniel Lloyd's book *Garden Craftsmanship in Yew and Box.* (Nathaniel Lloyd was the father of Christopher Lloyd of Great Dixter – topiary has always been a feature of that great English garden.) The topiary lawn at Earlshall Castle, in Fife, designed in his youth by the Scottish architect Sir Robert Lorimer, was a particular inspiration to Lloyd senior, and the Earlshall topiary was also the starting point for the Eythrope corner. The ivy-covered features can be seen as a modern spin on the vertical bedding that Miss Alice introduced when she chose her iron-framed birds, studded with plants, for Waddesdon and Eythrope.

POTS AROUND BUILDINGS

The pots near the Pavilion are spectacular in summer. The shadier side is dominated by twelve large orange pots, each one holding a column of white plumbago trained to five bamboos. The overall height of the display is almost 2.4 metres/8 feet. The plumbago, which flowers on new growth, has shoots that fall in long sprays from the main stems, so that the whole column foams with white flowers. The foot of each plumbago pillar rises from a mound of heliotrope 'Chatsworth' and this best of all scents hangs over the terrace. The heliotrope is also a key plant in the parterre and this link is important because it gives the area a unity of its own.

In addition to the large pots of plumbago and heliotrope, there are several smaller pots filled with the delicate nodding flowers of the white *Nicotiana suaveolens*. This Australian tobacco plant is deliciously scented and does not mind a little shade. It also seems resistant to the tobacco mosaic virus which has plagued other forms of *Nicotiana*. The repeated white in all the pots against a restrained planting of evergreen box billows and cut-leaf *Choisya* 'Aztec Pearl', along with the wonderful fragrance from the nicotiana and heliotrope, make this a cool and luxurious place to sit on a summer evening. Sometimes less variety really does mean more. Nan Fairbrother, one of the most influential English landscape architects of the twentieth century, was famous for saying 'sameness is all.' The restraint of this summer scheme for the terrace pots is a perfect illustration of that maxim.

The plumbagos are kept through the winter in a greenhouse which can take their full height. They are cut back to the bamboo frame at the end of the year, so that new growth will furnish the flowers for the following summer. Before the spring bedding of tulips and wallflowers goes in at the beginning of October, the soil in the pots is changed. The bulk of the compost is taken from the compost heaps where pumpkins have been grown, with a topping of the usual coir-based John Innes compost no. 2. A handful of seaweed meal is added to condition the soil, but the slow-release fertilizer that most gardeners now add to pots is not used. Attention to the exact needs of plants is, Sue thinks, critical. Heliotrope and plumbago perform better on high nitrogen than they might on an all-purpose mix. As a general rule the pot plants are given an initial feed of Vitax and then, starting from six weeks later, they are fed with a high-nitrogen fertilizer once a fortnight; but this can vary according to how the plant looks. The judgement of the gardener is equally important when it comes to watering. Three times a week is usually enough, but in hot weather they may need more and at rainy times less. This is something that the Eythrope gardeners have been trained to recognize. They say, 'You just know by looking at a plant what it needs.' When the pots are watered, it is done with a lance on the end of a hose and if you ask how much water should be given, the answer is that the hose stays over the pot until water runs out of the bottom.

Opposite
Pelargonium australe,
Heliotropium 'Dame Alice de Hales' and *Salvia* 'Wendy's Wish', at the corner of the potting shed.

The pots are crocked to improve drainage, although gardeners today are less likely to do this, as – in smaller pots than the ones used at Eythrope – crocking reduces the amount of compost available to the plants.

At the front of the house there is a sunnier aspect and here the planting is more Victorian in feeling and much more colourful. The scarlet 'Paul Crampel' geraniums that used to be set out in the parterre are now used in beds here, with the variegated *Pelargonium* 'Crystal Palace Gem' and the lime-green *Helichrysum petiolare* 'Limelight'. 'Paul Crampel' was introduced to England (from France) in 1892 and is a regular feature of the bedding outside Buckingham Palace. 'Crystal Palace Gem', introduced even earlier, in 1869, was named after Paxton's great glasshouse. It is likely that Miss Alice would have known and grown both of these Victorian favourites. Against the bright background *Abutilon* 'Canary Bird' is used as a feature plant in each pot, surrounded by more heliotrope 'Chatsworth'.

The stone urns that stand above the parterre complement the pink flowers of *Pelargonium* 'Lady Ilchester' and the silvery leaves of *P.* 'Grey Lady Plymouth' growing among billows of heliotrope 'Chatsworth'. The urns are filled with the variegated ivy-leaf *P.* 'Hederinum Variegatum' (syn. 'Duke of Edinburgh') in a slightly different pink, often placed around a centred cordyline. (Though the cordylines are raised from seed each year and can fail to germinate, so they do not always feature.) When plants do grow they go out from 12-cm/5-inch pots. The geraniums are planted from 9-cm/3½-inch pots. The urns are shallow, so larger plants would be hard to fit, but the cramped quarters do not affect performance because these plants are also fed regularly with high-nitrogen fertilizer.

The tubs in the courtyard that backs on to the walled garden have a changing plant palette. Here a planting that combines columns of blue plumbago and a larger variant of 'Paul Crampel' (see pages 10–11) has been much admired recently. This was a combination that Sue and Jonathan saw on a visit to Italy. In the past there has been a yellow scheme which included *Canna* 'Yellow Humbert', *Argyranthemum* 'Jamaica Primrose', *Bidens aurea* and *Helichrysum petiolare* 'Limelight'.

Whatever the plants chosen to furnish the different pots, dead-heading is vital. Not only does it keep plants in pristine form, it also encourages them to flower all summer.

POTS IN THE WALLED GARDEN

In high summer, the gravelled area in the corner of the walled garden is an enticing place. Here you can bask in the warm scent of heliotrope and study the many different plants growing in the array of pots. You can walk through the space and out the other side, winding through different clusters of pots arranged in colour groupings. Or you can pause on one of the Victorian fern-patterned iron seats and enjoy being at close quarters with so many horticultural beauties. Here the plants are grown as a single genus to a container, but they appear mixed, because as summer progresses the containers end up being completely hidden by foliage and flowers. The pot garden has its own atmosphere and once you are inside it is hard to remember that just beyond are rows of beans and cabbages.

The plants, which are all grown under glass, are set out at the end of May. Heliotrope 'Chatsworth' is used in bedding schemes around the house, but at least ten other heliotropes are raised each year at Eythrope and most of these end up dominating the pot garden. Heliotrope, or cherry pie, was a Victorian favourite for its vanilla-scented flowers. The garden historian Alice Coats writes that 'two of the Victorian varieties were characteristically named Miss Nightingale and Beauty of the Boudoir.' Many modern hybrids have more prosaic and masculine names (including 'W.H. Lowther', 'The Speaker' and 'Lord Roberts'), but there are some feminine ones too, as well as a couple named after the gardens where they were raised, like 'Gatton Park' and, of course, 'Chatsworth' itself. Today's hybrids range from white through mauve to the darkest purple 'Princess Marina', which is the least fragrant of them all. Perhaps the best scent comes from 'Chatsworth', 'White Lady' and 'W.H. Lowther'.

Heliotropes (officially *Heliotropium arborescens*) are sub-shrubs from South America, and they need sun and regular doses of a high-nitrogen fertilizer to flower well. They are frost-tender and should be propagated no later than the beginning of September, before the cold weather starts. At Eythrope cuttings are kept at a temperature no lower than 10°C/50°F throughout the winter. Old plants (apart from a few specimens of 'Chatsworth') are not kept, but more than six hundred cuttings of different varieties are taken annually each autumn. In gardens where there is not the space for such lavish propagation, established woody plants can be clipped over and reduced by about half and then lifted and put into containers. Kept dry in a frost-free house, they can be revived with watering and feeding once the weather warms up in the spring.

The other dominant flowers in the pot garden are argyranthemums in several shades, amaryllis, *Gladiolus murielae* and plenty of tall plants to give height and privacy. A large specimen of *Anisodontea* 'El Rayo', which is a dusty pink shrubby mallow, flowers all summer. The sky-blue *Sollya heterophylla* has tiny blue bells for months on end on

Opposite
Gladiolus murielae, with *Lavandula auriculata* × *christiana* and *Plumbago capensis*.

Opposite
Pots of tulip
'Apricot Parrot'.

Pages 232–233
Red *Salvia* 'Royal
Bumble' and magenta
S. microphylla 'Wild
Watermelon' with
Anisodontea 'El Rayo'.

a 1.8-metre/6-foot plant. There are giant daturas and, at the centre, a large deep red *Abutilon* 'Nabob' surrounded by dark purple heliotrope 'Princess Marina'. The colours are kept in groups: pale pinks and blues in one corner, sunset shades in another, with plenty of white throughout. One of the problems of associating plants in colonies of pots like this is that as they grow towards the light, they become one-sided. Careful pruning to balance the growth is, Sue thinks, better than turning the pots so that the bare growth can recover.

Many of the flowers keep going as long as they are deadheaded, but new arrivals also appear as summer passes. Later on, there will be added growth from pots of the white *Gladiolus murielae* and the unusual *Sinningia tubiflora. Sinningia* is related to the *Gloxinia* and is a little hard to flower. When it does, it produces small white tubular flowers which smell wonderful. The plant needs to be dormant in winter and kept in a frost-free place no hotter than 10°C/50°F, but in summer it likes to be hot and dry.

In the bed under the wall, where the peach case used to stand, is the nucleus of another collection of interesting plants. *Amaryllis belladonna* do well here and they can stay out all year. The white form of *Cobaea scandens* was used to cover the wall while new apples were trained to fill the space left after the glasshouse was demolished. *Cobaea* is a useful annual climber for hot walls and in a very warm place like this corner the seed ripens well in a hot summer.

In spring the focus of the pot garden shifts slightly, as it becomes an area to trial tulips. Growing tulips in pots is a good way to study their habit of flowering – how long the flowers last, how well they stand up to wind and rain, how useful they will be for picking or to plant in pots. All this research will influence future bulb orders. The pot garden in April becomes a library of tulips, providing an early blast of colour in the walled garden, before the high season of blossom and scent begins everywhere else.

THE TOPIARY GARDEN

The topiary-filled corner is very different from the highly coloured horticultural planting in the rest of the walled garden. Victorian in spirit but with a whimsical modernity, it has become a favourite feature. Box, yew and ivy, as well as golden *Lonicera nitida*, are all used to add texture and colour variation to the different cubes, pillars, orbs and animal shapes. It is a lively and amusing place, a complete contrast to the scale and order of everything else in the garden. Though the whole is a homage to the Lorimer design at Earshall Castle, there are no animals at Earshall. The animals here – the horses that started it off and the sheep frame that has been added – are a Rothschild addition.

At the beginning the pieces were set out on lawn, but mowing proved an intricate operation. At Lord Rothschild's suggestion, the grass was changed to a pale gravel to provide a better contrast to the green shapes. This was not totally successful and a darker stone was tried, with improved results. However, I thought that a red brick rubble might work even better, because it would chime with the building behind. Crushed bricks, which were often used in early bedding schemes, were introduced, with bands of grass left around the edges, near the box hedge which frames the topiary group. These changes, additions and refinements took several years to settle and perfect. It is rare for clients to understand that it can take time to work through the design process. The slow development of the design here provides a good illustration of how involved Lord Rothschild is with decisions of taste, and how patient he is until he feels something is right.

Box and yew need an annual trim and this is usually done in late summer, once growth has slowed. The area needs to be meticulously maintained to look good, and the work is demanding. Mechanical trimmers can be used on the large and simple shapes, but hand shears are better for the detailed work on orbs and animals. Lonicera is even more of a challenge. It is fast-growing, and troublesome if not kept tidy. At least three cuts a year are necessary to keep the bush solid and in the original shape. Ivy is done in winter, always using shears or secateurs, as it is important to cut through the stems rather than the leaves of any broad-leaved plant. A halved leaf is an ugly leaf.

Topiary is a good way of introducing solid forms among airy planting – think of topiary shapes as large green sculptures adding punctuation to a place. A single piece of topiary can be used in a small garden to great effect.

Opposite and pages 236–239
The topiary garden, where statues are surrounded by clipped shapes in box, yew and *Lonicera nitida* and by animal-shaped wire frames on which ivy is trained.

235

FLOWERS FOR THE HOUSE

FLORAL DECORATION

Cut flowers are never bought, even in winter. All year round there are flowers to pick for decoration. To modern eyes this might seem gloriously extravagant, but it was standard practice in every grand Victorian establishment. At Longleat in 1881, '30–40 button holes were needed daily in the darkest days of winter', as well as 'fourteen barrow loads of plants in flower (fine foliage and ferns count for nothing here) all through the dullest months'. At Waddesdon, Baron Ferdinand filled the house with palms and colourful variegated foliage plants. We know from the Waddesdon Manor Red Book that roses in vases of the same variety were used on the dining room table, together with trailing ferns, but when Miss Alice wrote to Johnson about 'my first and most important party at Waddesdon', to be held on Sunday 7 July 1907, she requested 'an abundant supply of fine fruit', but did not mention flowers. Vases of cut perennials in the Rothschild racing colours of blue and gold were sometimes used in Baron Ferdinand's day, although Mary Rose Blacker's *Flora Domestica*, the definitive study of historical flower arranging, suggests that mixing colours was not fashionable at that time.

When Miss Alice's great-nephew James and his wife inherited Waddesdon, they introduced more cut flowers. 'I don't think', wrote Mrs James, 'that any of Baron Ferdinand's guests visiting Waddesdon in our day would have noticed much difference in the arrangement of the rooms. The only major change was floral: instead of palms pervading the house, we substituted flowers, or flowering shrubs – a concession to modern taste.'

The Waddesdon arrangements in the era of Mrs James always involved very little foliage and this hangover from the high days of the Manor still prevails – even today foliage and pot plants are used sparingly. Maidenhair ferns grown in 18-cm/7-inch plastic pots may be crammed seven at a time into a trough to stand at the feet of statues in the conservatory area, and olive trees in pots also take a turn indoors, but the most stunning decoration comes from the metre-high floral arrangements which Sue does in the style which she was shown by Tim Hicks, who did the flowers for Mrs James both at the Pavilion and at the Manor. (He continued to arrange all the flowers until 1990.) He remembers that in Mrs James's day the best blooms always went to the Manor, where from March until October it was his job to decorate the house for visitors. At the Pavilion, Mrs James always had a big vase at the bottom of the staircase and one on her desk. Once, when guests were expected, he filled a showy vase with blue cornflowers and gold alstroemerias, in the tradition of the vases described in Baron Ferdinand's day, but was gently reproved when his employer said, 'We are not open to the public down here, you know.'

For guidance on floristry indoors, David Mlinaric, who advised on the interior at the Manor at the time of the 1990s restoration, was invaluable.

Page 240
An arrangement of dahlias 'Winston Churchill', 'Chat Noir' and 'Sam Hopkins' with *Leucanthemella serotina* (syn. *Chrysanthemum uliginosum*) and *Aster* 'Little Carlow'.

Opposite
Delphiniums are grown in quantity for cutting.

Pages 244–245
Freesias in an enamelled jar outside Sue's office.

It makes sense for anyone who grows their own flowers for picking to choose what will work with the colour schemes inside. At the Pavilion, flowers in tawny shades of orange, red and yellow suit one room. In others, softer pinky-mauve shades work best. Scented flowers are used as much as possible: freesias, hyacinths and narcissi all come indoors in winter but in summer care must be taken with sweet peas, because they can bring tiny insects with them. Lilies are rarely used, because some people are allergic to their pollen. Scented-leaf geraniums, grown in pots, appear at all times of year.

The weekly routine involves picking on Wednesday, for the weekend. The flowers are then conditioned by being left in buckets of water overnight. On Thursday morning Sue will arrange large set pieces on the spot. Smaller ones are arranged on the shelves outside her office and taken up to the house in the van. Vases usually need topping up over the weekend by whoever is on weekend duty. On Monday, all the flowers, including any pot plants, are removed, although any ferns and palms can be left indoors for up to six weeks without looking any the worse for wear.

The season starts with snowdrops. The early *Galanthus elwesii* 'Mrs Macnamara' is a great favourite: larger than the common *G. nivalis* and slightly scented, it looks wonderful in a glass vase on a dining table. Sometimes snowdrops are arranged on posy pads, which are 23-cm/9-inch plastic saucers designed to hold a circle of oasis. These are also used for small early wild daffodils like *Narcissus obvallaris* and *N. pseudonarcissus*, with moss to cover the oasis and sprigs of box around the edge.

The winter months are dependent on bulbs grown in pots. So many are grown that some are picked and combined with winter shrubs, while others are brought in as pot plants and placed in containers. Paperwhite narcissi furnish both Waddesdon and the Pavilion until Christmas, then hyacinths, followed by freesias and anemones, provide the mainstay from January until April. Tulips are also grown in pots in the frame yard for picking in April and May, and a special spring feature is a display of seventy auriculas in their pots on the hall table under the main staircase.

All summer, the cutting borders behind the greenhouse next to the orchard provide scented dianthus, Iceland poppies, foxgloves, peonies, zinnias and any new annuals that are being tried. Cosmos, dahlias, delphiniums, alstroemerias, antirrhinums and dark scabious are grown on the cut flower bank. The last flowers from the ground in the garden will be vases of hardy chrysanthemums and shocking pink nerines. Only very rarely are flowers in the borders picked, with the exception perhaps of the odd rose for a bedside table, or a tulip if a particular colour is in short supply from the bulbs that are grown in pots for picking.

For the show-stopping vases in the Waddesdon tradition, the flowers in season go into well-secured oasis, with a minimal backing of *Danaë racemosa* or box. In June, the outline might be made by thirty delphiniums and filled in with forty alstroemerias and as many foxgloves as will fit. It is always a matter of seeing what looks good. In a

Maidenhair ferns line the passage leading to the garden door.

Opposite
Zinnia Oklahoma Series, mixed. Zinnias, with their small flowers, are often picked for bedroom vases.

Pages 250 & 255
Single hollyhocks are grown from strains selected over years.

Pages 251–254
Dahlias flower until the first frosts. 'Jowey Mirella' and 'Sam Hopkins' are dramatic dark reds. Pink 'Gerrie Hoek' is an old favourite.

dry summer teasels and cosmos will provide enough material at a time when other flowers are fading. In September there might be an airier arrangement, with spiky dahlias 'Chat Noir' and plenty of Michaelmas daisies in season (perhaps the wonderful blue *Aster* 'Little Carlow'), or later in the year with chrysanthemums. The silvery pink 'Emperor of China', which is still in flower in November, is a particular favourite for late arrangements.

In addition to providing the flowers for the Pavilion and for London every week, the garden is often called upon to organize table arrangements for lunches at the Dairy. Twenty or thirty of these might be needed and they are usually done on posy pads. It is important to keep table decorations low, no higher than the start of the neck of a wine bottle, so that guests can see one another. A dazzling array of zinnias lined down a long table is particularly effective in late summer. Very occasionally the Manor is used for private parties and this too will mean more floristry, on a very grand scale. And every week bunches of Eythrope flowers will be made up for birthdays, or as a way of thanking someone, or for friends who are ill. These might be as rare as a bouquet of Malmaison carnations, or as lavish as a bunch of two hundred peonies for a distinguished visitor from the States.

DAHLIAS

By the beginning of the nineteenth century dahlias were, according to Loudon, 'the most fashionable flower in this country'. Their popularity lasted throughout the Victorian age, when they were often planted in the new perennial borders that were beginning to appear. Sometimes their tubers were eaten, but the passion for their glamorous flowers soon outweighed any appetite for cooking them. (Adventurous cooks say they taste like carrot and celery combined with potato.) In the Victorian country houses that went in for high floristry dahlias were regarded as indispensable cut flowers until the first frosts. In the twentieth century, though they continued to be grown in rows for picking in country houses like Rousham, and their rowdy colours were enjoyed in cottage gardens, they fell from favour with the horticultural cognoscenti. Vita Sackville-West was confident enough to grow a few dahlias at Sissinghurst, but it was only when Christopher Lloyd began to trumpet their virtues that these flamboyant flowers staged a proper comeback. Sarah Raven, the bold and brilliant gardener and flower arranger, has also been a great champion of dahlias, both in the garden and as cut flowers. Recently – and by this I mean in the last five years – articles proclaiming 'thank goodness dahlias are back in fashion' or headed 'How the once naff dahlia has made a dazzling comeback' have begun to appear in the horticultural press.

Dahlias have long been a feature of bedding schemes at Eythrope. Here they are as popular for picking from late July until the first frosts as they were in the nineteenth century. Over twenty different varieties are grown, with the bulk of the planting sited in the vinery border or on the cut flower bank. There, around ninety tubers are planted in blocks of fourteen, in rows 60 cm/2 feet apart. The 90-cm/3-feet wide paths for cultivating and picking run up the bank between the blocks of colour. Like much of the kitchen garden, in places where there is regular traffic for picking, the paths are strawed to keep the pickers' feet clean and the soil from compacting. The usual colour sequence on the bank is cerise, burgundy, lilac, yellow, orange and red.

In the frame yard there is another bed reserved for white, pale pink and some dark extras. Eight of each variety is the norm, but for a favourite (such as 'Winston Churchill' – a shocking pink that lights up any arrangement) the quantity is increased to a dozen. Sue also grows extra plants of a white Cactus variety from Rousham in the frame yard. Like all gardeners, she has an eye for a good specimen when she visits other gardens and often picks up unusual plants from other keen friends who are eager to swap plants. (Another good reason for exchanging plants is that it keeps rare things in circulation. If a plant packs up in one garden, it may well survive in a different setting.)

When the first frosts blacken the stems, which is usually at the end of October or in the first week of November, the dahlias are cut down and lifted for winter storage.

Opposite
Dahlias 'Chat Noir' and 'Ludwig Helfert', arranged in a liner that will be inserted in a china vase in the house.

Pages 258–259
Dahlia tubers are kept in pots of dry compost over the winter.

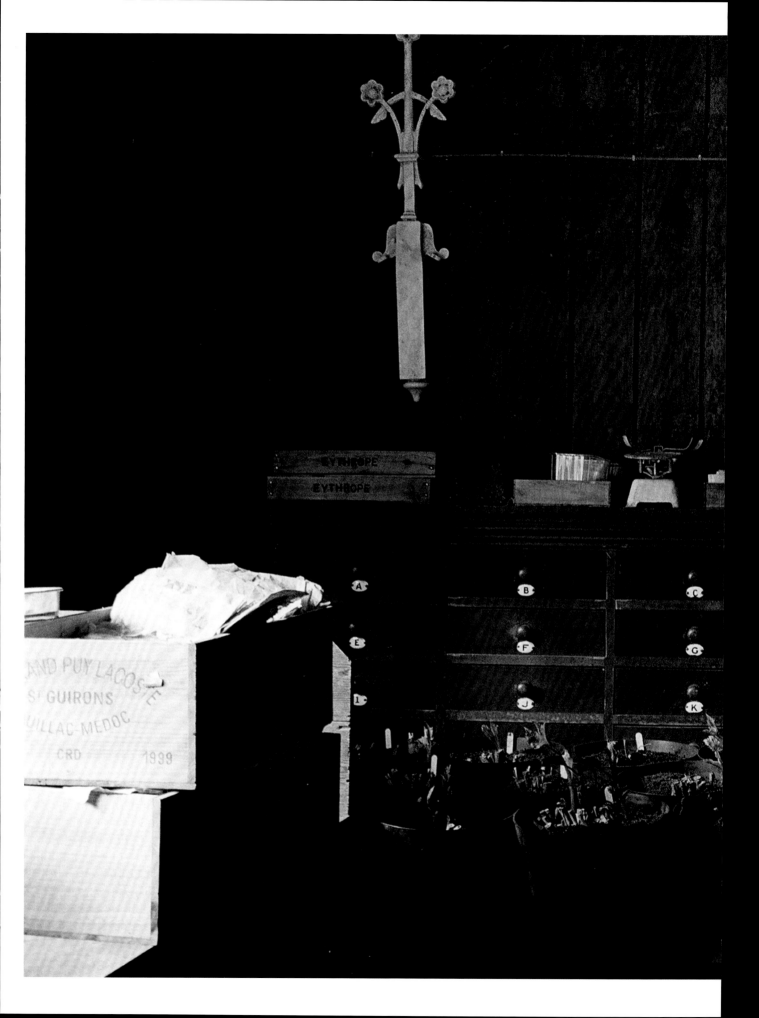

Cutting down dahlia stalks.

The stalks are cut in stages as netting is removed.

The clump of tubers is dug out.

Cleaned tubers ready to pot.

Dahlia tubers are kept dry over the winter, then watered in the spring.

The tubers are dried on the floor of the stable, upside down so that the stems can drain, and then after Christmas they are packed into coir compost in 25-cm/10-inch pots (well labelled to ensure that the bands of colour will be kept in strict order). This is a job to keep for bad weather days. A top dressing of leafmould is added at the end of January. The pots of tubers stay in the dark frost-free stable until the end of April or early May, depending on the weather. During the winter they are not watered, but they are checked once a month and any that show signs of shrivelling are moistened.

Once the dahlias go out into the frame yard, where they can be covered if late frosts threaten, they are watered regularly to start them growing again. The dahlia bed on the cut flower bank will have been prepared in the winter, when leafmould or well rotted manure is added, before the usual topdressing of seaweed meal and Vitax Q4 goes on to the beds. It will then be perfectly ready for the sprouted tubers to be planted at the beginning of June.

Staking dahlias is vital to stop the stems flopping, as in maturity they become very heavy and tend to fall apart. However, this is not done with individual stakes, which would be very time-consuming (they would probably need tying three times in a summer). Instead, on the cut flower bank the plants are grown through 15-cm/6-inch square plastic netting supported by forty stout posts (5 cm/2 inches square and 1.5 metres/5 feet high). By the time the plants are fully grown there will be three layers of netting about 30 cm/1 foot apart stretched tightly across the posts. This method also means the flowers are easier to pick, because the plants grow more loosely than they would if individually staked.

The most useful dahlias for cutting are Decoratives, Waterlilies and Cactus types. Individual dahlias are chosen for their colour and shape. For arranging, Sue likes thin stems, but the flowers must be open, although it is better if the anthers are not showing all over the centre. Picked in bud dahlias can wilt, because buds can prevent the stems from taking up water. A large late summer flower vase might include the dahlias 'Chat Noir', 'Rip City', 'Sam Hopkins', 'Jescot Nubia' and the bright cerise 'Winston Churchill', with *Leucanthemella serotina* and *Aster* 'Little Carlow' towards the edge of the arrangement.

SEED-RAISED ANNUALS,
BIENNIALS AND PERENNIALS

Biennials, annuals and plenty of dianthus are all grown for cutting. As the last tulips fade, foxgloves and sweet williams will take their place for indoor arrangements. Both are sown in the propagating house, as this allows control over numbers and is easier to manage than risky open-ground sowing. They are sown in May, in seed trays, and pricked out and potted on into 9-cm/3½-inch pots. They struggle a little at the leap from tray to pot, but soon establish in a coolish shaded greenhouse. There will be a hundred of each to plant out in July or early August. In early summer of the following year, the foxgloves (usually *Digitalis purpurea* f. *albiflora*, although *D. purpurea* 'Pam's Choice' is a recent addition) will be ready for picking. They can be relied on to fill large vases, along with pyrethrum and later with delphiniums and alstroemerias.

The sweet williams are needed for smaller scented posies in May. They are the auricula-eyed forms, although only 50 per cent of the doubles, which are preferred, will germinate in each batch. Voles are also a problem for sweet williams, as in some years they eat the stems at ground level.

Iceland poppies are sown later in the year, generally towards the end of July. They are sown in plugs, as they dislike being pricked out and transplanted, and this way the transition to 9-cm/3½-inch pots is gentler. These will be planted out in September and will be ready to pick from late spring the following year over a long season. If they are sown earlier than July, they can start flowering too soon – in the autumn of the same year. The strain grown is selected and regularly rogued from the Constance Finnis Group, which includes more pastel colours than the ordinary type and has good long stems. Any poppies that appear in hot oranges or strong yellows are removed and half of the white flowers are also culled, as white can become too dominant.

The annuals for cutting always include zinnias. Sown in May in plugs under glass to avoid any check to their growth, they germinate very fast. By the time they are ready to be hardened off and lined up outside in the spaces between the glasshouses, all risk of cool weather will be past. The varieties chosen are mixed cultivars of Benary's Giant Series and Oklahoma Series, as well as the smaller Sprite Group, which is often more resistant to a rainy summer than the larger hybrids. Like most of the plants at Eythrope, the zinnias are conditioned with seaweed meal and fed with Vitax Q4.

Another reliable annual is the dark, almost black, *Scabiosa atropurpurea* 'Ace of Spades', which is grown not from seed but from cuttings, which ensures it flowers earlier. Cuttings are taken in the autumn, when huge numbers of plants are propagated for the following year. At the Pavilion the scabious is often arranged in tall celery vases or used in table decorations.

Planting out annuals.

Precise spacing.

Firming in the plants.

Cane supports for delphiniums.

Boards are used to keep the soil from getting compacted.

Blocks of oasis are firmly tied down in the vase and soaked.

Airy *Aster pilosus* var. *pringlei* 'Monte Cassino' provides a background.

The edges are filled with box foliage.

The main display of *Echinops ritro* forms the shape. Phlox is added last.

Echinops ritro, cosmos and scabious 'Ace of Spades' ready to go to the house to be used in arrangements.

Opposite
The arrangement of
Echinops ritro and
Phlox maculata 'Alpha',
backed by *Aster pilosus*
var. *pringlei* 'Monte
Cassino', which is
shown being created
on the previous pages.

Scented flowers are always in demand for picking. Sweet peas are invaluable. The Spencer multiflora types are sown in October in John Innes no. 2 compost made with coir, one seed to each root trainer. In order to foil mice and woodlice, which can be a nuisance, they are germinated in a frost-free glasshouse (at 5°C/41°F) rather than in a frame. The plants are pinched out when they reach two leaves and will be hardened off in a cold house at the beginning of March so that they can be planted out at the end of the month. They will then be ready to pick in May. Particular house favourites are 'Chatsworth', 'Noel Sutton', 'Elizabeth Taylor', 'Leamington', 'Southbourne' and 'Anniversary', but as with all the flowers grown, new varieties are tried and advice is often sought from specialist growers. The old-fashioned pre-Spencer varieties, which are even more scented than the modern forms, are sown after Christmas and planted out in May. The deep purple bicolour 'Matucana', cerise 'Prince Edward' and the pink and white 'Painted Lady' are popular.

Sweet peas do not have a long vase life – their colour and scent usually fade within a couple of days. Sue has adopted the Japanese practice of adding sugar to the water, in the proportion of 100g to 1 litre. This has had a dramatic effect on vase life (the sweet peas now last for up to six days), and oasis posy pads have also been soaked in the solution with similar results. Pollen beetles can be a nuisance indoors when they leave the flowers and move towards the light, so after cutting, the sweet peas are left in a dark place with one source of light, so that by the time they go into the house the beetles have flown. Another way of dealing with these insects is to fill a yellow bucket with water and stand it next to the row of sweet peas. The beetles are attracted to the colour yellow and then drown themselves in the water.

Pinks are essential for summer picking but they need to be renewed before two seasons of growth are over. Young plants produce the best flowers, because once the stems get woody, the numbers of flowers decline, so half of the pink bed is replaced each year. Cuttings are not taken until September, but they root without heat and are ready to go out after a winter spent in a cold greenhouse. The repeat-flowering forms 'Rose de Mai', 'Red Welsh', 'Moulin Rouge' and 'Laced Joy' are favourites for their long season, but as many as eighty-two varieties have been grown and trialled at Eythrope, so there is always a scented bunch to be picked from May until October. It is a popular assumption that pinks, being chalk-lovers, will thrive in poor, dry conditions, but the dianthus bed is well watered in times of drought and fed with Vitax, so that the plants do well and yield plenty of long-stemmed flowers.

CHRYSANTHEMUMS

Chrysanthemums were always the autumn flower of choice to decorate the Victorian house. Samuel Broome wrote in 1857 that the introduction of the pompon varieties 'has tended in no small degree to resuscitate the cultivation of the Chrysanthemum.' And Alice M. Coats, our greatest flower historian, suggests that the larger kinds became more popular after Robert Fortune brought some back to England from Japan in 1861. But it was not until the end of the century that they were widely grown at the large estates. Rows of them in pots can be seen in old pictures of the Paradise garden at Waddesdon, so we know they were in use there. Like dahlias, chrysanthemums later fell out of fashion – perhaps because they were so often the flower of choice for funerals. But just as dahlias are today considered eminently desirable garden plants, chrysanthemums are also having a moment. The hardier sorts are now being grown again, mainly for picking, and at Eythrope they are relied on for indoor arrangements from September to November.

While gardeners of Miss Alice's day filled glasshouses with displays of enormous blooms that could be admired on a garden tour, or brought inside for the elaborate table decorations, the modern tendency is for looser, simpler arrangements. The hardy outdoor types, which can be in flower until the worst frosts start, are used as sprays and can last as long as a fortnight in the house. Sue is always looking for late-flowering varieties which will stand mild frosts. After consulting the holder of the National Collection of Chrysanthemums, who is also a flower arranger, she recently bought 'Uri', which is pink. Tried and tested outdoor types are 'Bretforton Road', a good purple, 'Ruby Mound', the white 'Wedding Day', and – loveliest and latest of all to flower – 'Emperor of China', which is pink with silvery quills and completely hardy. If there is room for only one chrysanthemum this is the one to suit most gardeners, but, at 1.5 metres/5 feet, it is rather tall.

At Eythrope the last picking of the year is usually around the second week of November, but with luck the flowers will still be looking good a fortnight later. Naomi, who is responsible for cut flowers, observes that it is best to pick the chrysanthemums in bud, before they get frosted or ruined by rain, because they will always open well in the heat of the house. Towards the end of the season, they are lifted and brought into a cold glasshouse to extend flowering for as long as possible. Once flowering stops, the plants are cut down. Ten of each variety are then potted to be brought into a frost-free glasshouse until early or mid-January, when they are moved to a warmer glasshouse with a temperature of 5°–10°C/40°–50°F so that the shoots start to grow from the base. Once that has happened cuttings are taken. When the shoots are 2.5–5 cm/1–2 inches tall, they are used as soft tip cuttings, which are dipped in hormone rooting powder (this needs to be fresh) and then packed, twenty at a time, into half-size seed trays in a 50/50

mix of coco fibre and perlite. They root best at 5°–10°C/40°–50°F, but no bottom heat is used. Jonathan and Naomi, who are in charge of all the propagating, prefer to cover the cuttings with white polythene sheeting which is turned twice a day until roots have formed, which usually takes about three weeks. The new plants are then potted individually into 9-cm/3½-inch pots in a John Innes no. 2 mix (made with coco fibre instead of peat) and returned to the propagating house with a temperature of 10°C/50°F for a couple of weeks, until they have rooted again.

Hardened off in a frame in April and then stood outside during May, the plants are ready to go in the ground by the end of May or in early June. They are grown in narrow beds through plastic netting, like the dahlias. The only likely problem, Jonathan says, is white rust. Plants will usually escape this so long they are grown without check from lack of water, but it is important to keep an eye out for it in August and September when growth is rapid and flower buds are forming. Chemical control is possible but, as Jonathan says, prevention is better than cure. There is rarely any need to resort to pesticides when plants are kept healthy from the start of their lives, and the gardener is watchful – always.

BULBS IN POTS

All through the winter the garden provides a succession of bulbs in pots for flowers to decorate the house. The bulb order is always completed in July. (It is worth ordering early, to be sure that chosen varieties are not sold out.) The growing season starts when the bulbs for forcing arrive in September, before the main bulb order is delivered a month later.

At Eythrope, the boxes containing bulbs of paperwhites, hyacinths, freesias and anemones will be unpacked around the middle of September and soon after that the first of the paperwhite narcissi will be potted up so that they will be in flower for November and early December. Hundreds of bulbs of *Narcissus* 'Ziva' are planted eight to ten to each 18-cm/7-inch pot in equal parts of John Innes no. 2 and coco fibre and then covered with mypex for about a fortnight. The enforced darkness is important, as without a good root system the bulbs will not perform properly. But paperwhites come through fast. They should never be made too wet. They are left in the frames and if the weather is mild will sometimes flower without being moved to a warmer place. Once the frosts start and flowers out of doors begin to be scarce, the pots of bulbs are brought into the cherry house, where the glass provides protection from the worst weather; there is no heat but plenty of light. Most of the paperwhites are grown for picking and these will be staked in a workmanlike way, but those that are destined to go indoors in bowls will be staked with lime twigs and raffia. Further plantings are made in fortnightly succession and treated in the same way. The first planting will be out by the beginning of November and paperwhites will be used to decorate the various houses, either as cut flowers or in containers, right through to the beginning of March.

Prepared hyacinths, which are slower to flower than the paperwhites, are planted at around the same time, but these are potted up in 9-cm/3½-inch individual pots, in potting compost, and covered with a 10-cm/4-inch layer of coco fibre and then with newspaper to keep them dark under the frames for about six weeks. The lids of the frames are open as much as possible, but kept shut in heavy rain or snow. Growing hyacinths singly makes it easier to choose bulbs at matching stages of growth to be put into the baskets or tins that will end up in fine containers indoors. Once the hyacinths' roots have developed, the bulbs are brought into an unheated glasshouse for a week, until the leaves begin to green. They are then moved to frost-free glass for another week and finally to a warmer house (heated to 10°C/50°F) to be ready for Christmas. Hyacinths are generally better grown slowly – that way they never get straggly and drawn. However, if you want to keep them on hold, they do need to get to a point where the tip of the flower is showing some colour, before they can be returned to a cooler temperature. 'Pink Pearl' and 'White Pearl' are two unvarying favourites for forcing for Christmas, because they have neat leaves and compact flowers with green buds. The flowers are airy and often produce two spikes to a bulb.

Opposite
Paperwhite *Narcissus* 'Ziva'. Paperwhites are grown in pots for picking.

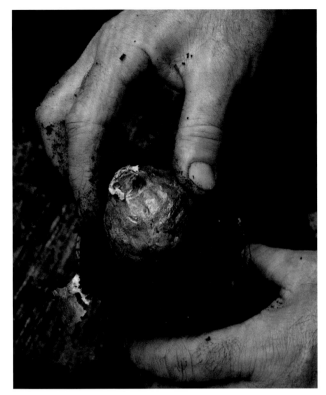

Hyacinth bulbs are half-buried.

Clear labelling and keeping bulbs in separate groups is a help.

In the cold frame bulbs are covered in coco fibre to encourage roots to form first.

The frame is kept open most of the time, and only closed when it rains.

When the bulbs come from the frame into a cold glasshouse they are covered with newspaper for a week.

Bamboos support freesias.

Freesias are always used as cut flowers, as their growth is untidy even when staked.

After the Christmas batch of prepared bulbs, ordinary hyacinths continue to be used for decoration through January until April. There are old favourites, like 'Woodstock', 'Blue Jacket' and 'City of Haarlem', but every year a few new varieties are tried, to see if they are worth growing. (Trialling any plant is a useful exercise for all gardeners. The flower you see at a show or in a magazine will never be quite the same as the one grown under more realistic conditions at home. The best way to judge a plant is to see it growing in conditions similar to your own.)

In the past, all the hyacinths grown for decorating the house were staked with lime twigs. Hyacinths can be very top heavy, although if you choose the smallest (size one) bulbs, or grow Roman hyacinths, which are more delicate, the staking need not be quite so strong. Recently Sue has experimented with using individual kebab sticks, rather than lime twigs. The sticks are stabbed into the bulb behind the flowering stem and neatly tied to the flower stalk with raffia. This is almost invisible. All the bulbs that are brought indoors are 'mossed'. Moss is collected from the woods and kept damp in a plastic bag until it is needed. It adds the finishing touch to a scented bowl of forced spring bulbs.

Freesias are another winter flower used to decorate the various houses. The corms are prepared to plant and flower at particular times of the year. The temperature has a profound effect on the development and flowering of freesias. Those planted in September will flower in February, provided the temperature can be kept at 15°C/60°F for the first six weeks and then at 10–12°C/50–55°F. They are planted nine at a time, in a 12-cm/5-inch pot in potting compost with the nose of the corm showing above soil surface.

Like the hyacinths and narcissi, they used to start life by spending a month in the cold frame before being brought into the heated glasshouse at a temperature of 8–10°C/45–50°F. (This is the critical temperature at which they form flower buds. Too warm and the buds fail to appear.) They should be in flower in February and March but some years they were later, which caused problems as they were taking up the space needed to grow on all the half-hardy bedding for the borders. So now, to ensure they are ready earlier, they start life in the glasshouse.

Individual colours are chosen rather than a mix, with more yellow and white than other colours, as these have the best scent. Some red and purple are also sown. (Red is a cheerful colour in the winter months but its scent is less good than that of the paler varieties.) All the freesias sown are single forms and all need staking very carefully with thin green canes and raffia, once the leaves are about 10 cm/4 inches tall, but they rarely end up indoors in pots, as their leaves are so untidy. Like the paperwhites they are mostly used for picking. Freesias are useful for bedroom arrangements and table decorations. They also make good bouquets, but they are better kept in bunches of ten stems at a time, as they can get very muddled.

The last to flower of the early bulb delivery are the de Caen anemones (not strictly bulbs, but corms). Anemones are not grown in pots, but in an uncovered frame in the frame yard for picking.

Opposite
The flamed cherry and white tulip 'Estella Rijnveld'.

Pages 282–283
Flower-arranging props.

Opposite
Crates of potted bulbs
waiting to go into the
cold frames.

They are planted in September and are usually ready to pick in March and April. In mild winters they survive to flower the following year and do not need reordering. For picking, the named varieties are better than the mixed bags on offer. Red 'Hollandia', blue 'Mister Fokker', soft purple 'Sylphide' and white 'The Bride' have all proved easy and colourful for a long season in the winter months, but all picked anemones are thirstier than any other cut flowers, so their vases need refilling regularly.

Tulip bulbs are also grown in the frame yard in pots for picking. This means that their flowering can be speeded up if they are needed for a particular date. Twenty of each variety are planted in 25-cm/10-inch pots in November and it is important that they are well watered in that first month. They are staked with canes and raffia to keep the stems straight for arranging indoors. The types chosen are designed to provide a rainbow of colours for cutting from April until the end of May. Some favourites are the scented early 'Bellona', the striped 'Helmar' and 'Happy Generation', which are like old Rembrandt tulips seen in Dutch still-life paintings, and several of the fringed late sorts. The early Fosterianas are not grown because their flowers are too big, and only a few Parrots because some of them have weak stems. Some of the most useful and elegant tulips, Sue judges, are the single late varieties in a classic egg shape which keep going until the end of May. The white 'Maureen' and black 'Queen of Night' are especially popular.

Snowdrop

A pale and pining girl, head bowed, heart gnawed,
whose figure nods and shivers in a shawl
of fine white wool, has suddenly appeared
in the damp woods, as mild and mute as snowfall.
She may not last. She has no strength at all,
but stoops and shakes as if she'd stood all night
on one bare foot, confiding with the moonlight.

One among several hundred clear-eyed ghosts
who get up in the cold and blink and turn
into these trembling emblems of night frosts,
she brings her burnt heart with her in an urn
of ashes, which she opens to re-mourn,
having no other outlet to express
her wild-flower sense of wounded gentleness.

Yes, she's no more now than a drop of snow
on a green stem—her name is now her calling.
Her mind is just a frozen melting glow
of water swollen to the point of falling,
which maybe has no meaning. There's no telling
But what a beauty, what a mighty power
of patience kept intact is now in flower.

POSTSCRIPT

It is twenty-five years since we came to live at Eythrope and began our garden, and this book is a testament to the people who helped us make it. Mary Keen, the author, designed the garden and it was she who found for us Sue Dickinson, our resident genius of whom it was said, by Robin Lane Fox, that had she played at Wimbledon she would have been seeded no.1.

Over the years many changes have been made – a flock of chickens in the orchard, a golden cupola added to the rose arbour, poems on slate tablets written in silver by Alice Oswald, who worked here for a while, statues dropped here and there, a topiary parterre with red gravel carefully chosen to mirror the garden buildings, an auricula theatre of silvered oak, a plashing fountain with frogs and lily pads, and much more besides.

I hope this book will give pleasure and of course instruction to all who read it.

Jacob Rothschild
Serena Rothschild
Eythrope, 23 November 2014

APPENDICES

Appendix 1: The Gardeners

SUE DICKINSON was one of the last girl gardeners to train at Waterperry under Miss Havergal, from 1969 to 1971. Her first job, as a trainee, was in Ireland, at Malahide Castle. The garden she remembers as 'Tasmania in Ireland'. After a year there, at Lord Talbot's suggestion, she moved to the Belgian garden and arboretum at Kalmthout, where she learned about trees and propagation. This was followed by a couple of years at the new Reading Botanic Garden, which she found especially interesting because it was being started from scratch. In a field. A short spell at Hatfield followed, until she spotted the chance to work at Sissinghurst. Three years with Pam Schwerdt and Sibylle Kreutzberger taught her about plant association and how to make the best of a garden by feeding (and dead-heading). Seven years with Mrs Merton at Burghfield Old Rectory followed. Esther Merton was a famous gardener who was mad about plants and growing things to cook. Sue reflects that much of her gardening has been learned from women who were passionate about flowers and cooking. Finally she moved, with all the experience of her varied horticultural posts, to Eythrope, where she has now been for twenty-five years.

JONATHAN COOKE is a vicar's son. His academic parents, who met at Oxford, both loved gardening. After a spell at Durham University, reading sociology and archaeology, he decided that academic work was not for him and he left to go to Pershore to learn about horticulture. This was followed by three years at Wye College. He spent ten years at Waterperry Gardens as assistant manager and then moved to being in charge of the important restoration work of the gardens at the Baroque Castle Bromwich. He came to Eythrope twelve years ago, as assistant head gardener to Sue, with whom he now lives. Jonathan's particular responsibility is for propagation but he is also involved in the overall look of the place.

PAUL CALLINGHAM's father, Jack, was head gardener to Mrs James de Rothschild, so he grew up at Eythrope. He began to work as a gardener there as soon as he left school at sixteen. After this gardening start under his father, he thought he wanted to try something different and he left to work in a sheet metal factory. A year indoors convinced him that what he really loved was working outside, and he came home to Eythrope, where he has now been gardening for thirty years. Paul's special responsibilities are vegetable growing, and the growing of freesias under glass. He says that for almost all the year he spends a couple of days a week harvesting the crops he grows. Eythrope has been his life, as it was his father's.

THOMAS BAIRD left school at sixteen and went to Askham Bryan College in Yorkshire to study horticulture. He did well, earning distinctions for his diplomas, and then he went to Le Manoir aux Quat' Saisons in Oxfordshire, where he worked for six years. He loves gardening at Eythrope and particularly enjoys seed sowing and pruning. In his spare time he makes jam from everything, including the fruit of *Cornus mas*.

BARRY CLARKE started life as a builder, but his parents were keen gardeners who grew flowers and vegetables, especially potatoes. 'Foremost' early potatoes and 'The Sutton' broad beans are still his favourites. Barry does all the mowing round the Pavilion. The fine mowing takes almost two days a week in summer. He is also responsible for watering the pots, which needs sensitive judgement.

NAOMI CORBOULD was brought up in a family of keen gardeners. Her mother sold vegetable seeds to her children, but she bought the produce that they grew. Naomi read biology at Leeds University and then worked in a bank for ten years, while cultivating an allotment. She then retrained as a gardener at Askham Bryan, although at the time she was not sure that gardening was a job she could do for life. A Harold Hillier apprenticeship, followed by a year in New Zealand at the Wellington Botanic Garden, convinced her that she could. She planned to stay in New Zealand, but when her mother got ill she returned to England. She has been at Eythrope for six years. Naomi is the cut flower gardener and she also looks after the ferns. She loves being busy all day outside and working with nature.

JONATHAN SHEFFORD left Eythrope in the summer of 2014 and is now head gardener at a private garden in Kent. After leaving school at sixteen he started his working life at Chequers. He then moved on to work for Lord Heseltine before starting his time at Eythrope. Growing auriculas and Malmaisons and clipping topiary were the things he particularly enjoyed, but he says that everything about gardening is his passion, and he can't imagine doing anything else.

DAVE MEADS left school to garden at Eythrope for Mrs James de Rothschild for three years, but then he went into factory work and moved to Suffolk to get married. He kept up with gardening on Saturdays for his brother-in-law, who was a landscape contractor. When a job came up in 2003, Paul, who has been a lifelong friend, suggested he should return to Eythrope. Dave enjoys hedges and mowing as well as being in charge of the pelargonium house. He says he likes all aspects of gardening – even in bad weather. In his free time, he enjoys walking his dog in the park.

TIM SIMMONDS worked locally as a shepherd for four years before starting on the estate as a farm worker. When he changed to gardening he was surprised by how like ploughing mowing is: you need a straight eye for both. He shares the mowing with Barry and is the man who understands machinery.

ALICE OSWALD, the poet, worked at Eythrope as a gardener for two years after leaving Oxford and spending a year at Wisley, followed by two more with the National Trust at Cliveden. During her time as a gardener, she wrote several poems and some of these, written on slates with a silver pen, are propped against the wall in the passage that leads into the garden. She says: 'It was wonderful to come across someone as devoted to her work as Sue. Plants seemed actually excited by her presence. She taught me a lot about gardens, but perhaps she taught me even more about patience and concentration. She has remained a lifelong friend.'

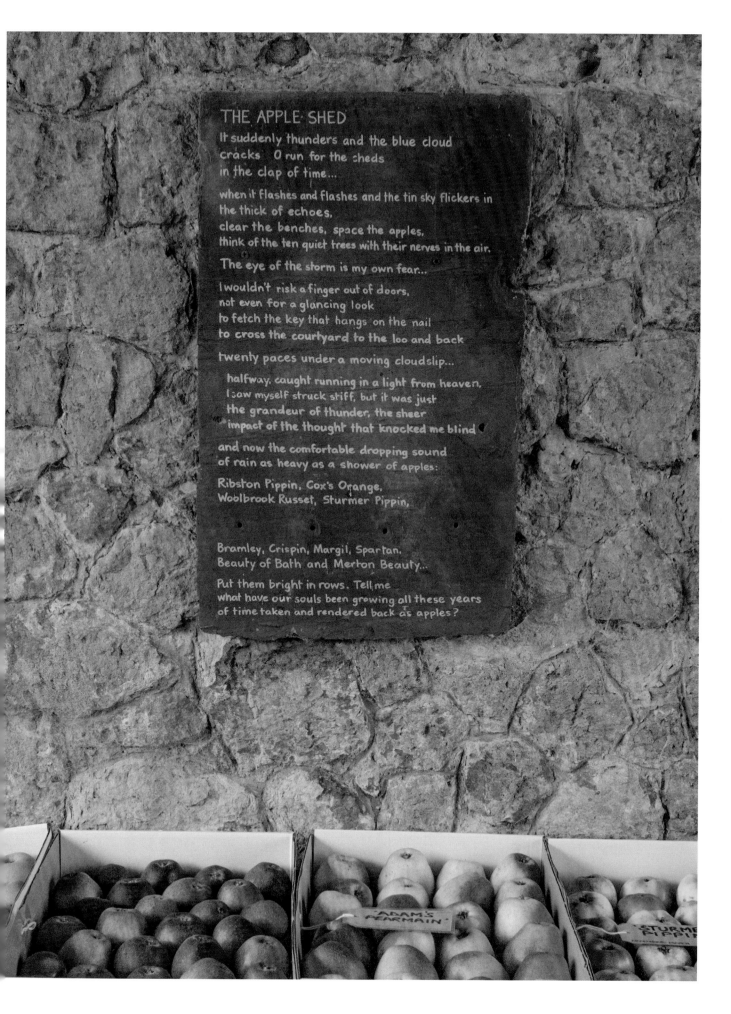

THE APPLE SHED

It suddenly thunders and the blue cloud
cracks   O run for the sheds
in the clap of time...

when it flashes and flashes and the tin sky flickers in
the thick of echoes,
clear the benches, space the apples,
think of the ten quiet trees with their nerves in the air.

The eye of the storm is my own fear...

I wouldn't risk a finger out of doors,
not even for a glancing look
to fetch the key that hangs on the nail
to cross the courtyard to the loo and back

twenty paces under a moving cloudslip...

halfway, caught running in a light from heaven,
I saw myself struck stiff, but it was just
the grandeur of thunder, the sheer
impact of the thought that knocked me blind

and now the comfortable dropping sound
of rain as heavy as a shower of apples:

Ribston Pippin, Cox's Orange,
Woolbrook Russet, Sturmer Pippin,

Bramley, Crispin, Margil, Spartan,
Beauty of Bath and Merton Beauty...

Put them bright in rows. Tell me
what have our souls been growing all these years
of time taken and rendered back as apples?

Appendix 2:

Vegetables and fruit from the walled garden

JANUARY
Broccoli, purple sprouting 'Rudolph'
Cabbage 'January King'
Cabbage, red
Cabbage, Savoy
Cabbage, white (coleslaw type)
Celeriac
Garlic
Herbs: bay, coriander, dill, mint, parsley, rosemary, thyme
Jerusalem artichokes (last)
Kale, curly
Kale, black ('Nero di Toscana', *cavolo nero*)
Corn salad (lamb's lettuce) (last)
Leeks
Onions (last)
Parsnips
Potatoes, maincrop, red & white (last)
Rocket
Shallots
Sprouts
–
Apples

FEBRUARY
Broccoli, purple sprouting
Broccoli, white sprouting
Cabbage 'January King'
Cabbage, red
Cabbage, Savoy
Celeriac
Garlic
Herbs: mint, parsley, rosemary, tarragon, thyme
Jerusalem artichokes
Leeks
Shallots
–
Apples

MARCH
Broccoli, sprouting, purple & white
Cabbage, spring
Garlic
Herbs: bay, coriander, dill, mint, parsley, rosemary, sorrel, thyme
Rocket
Seakale
Spinach (beet, not annual)
Swiss chard
–
Rhubarb

APRIL
Asparagus (3rd week April)
Cabbage, spring
Herbs: bay, coriander, dill, mint, parsley, rosemary, sorrel, thyme
Seakale
Spinach
Swiss chard
Rocket
–
Rhubarb

MAY
Asparagus
Beans, broad (4th week May)
Herbs: basil (under glass, 4th week May), bay, chives, coriander, dill, mint, parsley, rosemary, sorrel, thyme
Lettuce
Rocket
Spinach
Swiss chard
–
Rhubarb

JUNE
Asparagus (until 2nd week June)
Beetroot, baby (towards end June)
Beans, broad
Carrots, baby (towards end June)
Cucumber (mid-June)
Fennel (end June)
Garlic
Herbs: basil, bay, chives, coriander, dill, mint, parsley, rosemary, sorrel, thyme
Leeks, baby
Lettuce
Peas
Potatoes, new (2nd week June)
Shallots
Spring onions
–
Gooseberries (early June)
Rhubarb
Strawberries (3rd week June)

JULY
Aubergines
Beans, broad
Beans, French
Beetroot, red, yellow, white & purple
Cabbage, summer round
Calabrese
Carrots
Courgettes
Cucumbers
Fennel
Garlic
Globe artichokes
Herbs: borage, basil, chives, coriander, dill, edible flowers, parsley, savory, sorrel, thyme
Leeks, baby
Lettuce, 'Little Gem', purple lettuce, salad leaves, cabbage lettuce
Onions
Peas
Peppers
Potatoes, new & salad
Shallots
Spinach
Spring onions
Swiss chard
Tomatoes, cherry & large (3rd/4th week)
Turnips
–
Apricots
Blackberries
Blackcurrants
Figs
Peaches
Redcurrants
Strawberries
Strawberries, wild
Whitecurrants

AUGUST
Aubergines
Beans, French
Beans, runner, 'Hunter'
Beetroot (red, yellow, white, purple)
Cabbage
Calabrese
Carrots
Courgettes
Cucumbers
Fennel
Garlic
Globe artichokes
Herbs: basil, borage, chives, coriander, dill, edible flowers, parsley, savory, sorrel, thyme
Kale, black (*cavolo nero*)
Leeks, baby
Lettuce
Marrow 'Vegetable Spaghetti'
Onions, white & red
Peas
Pepper
Potatoes, salad
Shallots
Sweet corn
Spinach
Spring onions
Swiss chard
Tomatoes, cherry & large
Turnips
–
Apricots
Blackberries
Greengages
Nectarine
Peaches
Plums
Raspberries
Strawberries, wild

SEPTEMBER
Aubergines (harvested and trayed up to clear house for propagation)
Beans, dwarf French, 'Safari'
Beans, French
Beans, runner
Beetroot, red, yellow, white & pink
Cabbage, round summer
Cabbage, Savoy
Calabrese
Carrots
Celeriac
Courgettes
Cucumbers
Fennel
Garlic
Globe artichokes
Herbs: basil, borage, chives, coriander, dill, edible flowers, garlic chives, mint, parsley, rosemary, sage, savory, sorrel, tarragon, thyme, Welsh onion, winter savory
Kale, black, 'Nero di Toscana'
Leeks
Leeks, baby
Lettuce, mixed salad leaves & 'Little Gem' type
Marrow 'Vegetable Spaghetti'
Onions
Peppers (harvested and trayed up to clear house for propagation)
Potatoes (in sacks, already lifted in early August)
Salad 'Juliette', 'Anya'
Maincrop, red & white
Shallots (dried off in greenhouse, cleaned and kept in trays in cool shed)
Spinach
Spring onions
Sweet corn
Swiss chard
Tomatoes, cherry & large
Turnips
–
Apples, cooking & dessert
Blackberries
Damsons
Figs
Grapes
Melons
Pears, cooking & dessert
Plums
Quinces
Raspberries
Strawberries, wild

OCTOBER
Beans, runner
Beetroot
Cabbage, red
Cabbage, Savoy
Cabbage, white, coleslaw type
Calabrese
Cauliflower, Romanesco
Celeriac
Endive, Radicchio
Fennel
Garlic
Herbs: basil, chives, coriander,
    dill, mint, parsley, savory,
    sorrel, tarragon, thyme
Kale, black (*cavolo nero*)
Kale, curly
Leeks, large
Lettuce
Onions
Pepper, green & red
Potatoes, salad & maincrop, red
    & white
Pumpkin
Salad leaves
Shallots
Spinach
Spring onions
Sprouts
Swede
Swiss chard
Squash
Tomatoes, cherry & large
–
Apples, cooking and dessert
Figs
Grapes
Pears, cooking and dessert
Quince
Damsons
Raspberries

NOVEMBER
Beetroot
Cabbage, red
Cabbage, Savoy
Cabbage, white
Cauliflower, Romanesco
Celeriac
Chinese artichokes
Corn salad (lamb's lettuce)
Endive, Radicchio
Fennel
Garlic
Herbs: chives, mint, parsley,
    sorrel, tarragon, thyme
Jerusalem artichokes
Kale, black (*cavolo nero*)
Kale, curly
Leeks
Lettuce
Marrow 'Vegetable Spaghetti'
Onions
Parsnips
Potatoes, maincrop
Pumpkin

Shallots
Rocket
Spinach
Sprouts
Squash
Swede
Swiss chard
–
Apples, cooking and dessert
Pears, cooking and dessert
Quince

DECEMBER
Cabbage 'January King'
Cabbage, red, 'Rodina', 'Marner
    Lagerrot'
Cabbage, Savoy, 'Endeavour',
    'Tundra'
Cabbage, white coleslaw,
    Holland Winter White
Celeriac 'Monarch', 'Prinz'
Corn salad (lamb's lettuce)
Endive, Radicchio
Garlic 'Silent Night'
Herbs: coriander, dill (under
    glass), parsley, mint,
    rosemary (outside), sage,
    tarragon, thyme
Jerusalem artichokes
Kale, curly dwarf
Kale, black, 'Nero di Toscana'
Leeks 'Tadorna', 'Toledo',
    'Atlanta', 'Oarsman'
Lettuce, last
Onions
Parsnips 'Gladiator', 'Palace'
Potatoes, maincrop, red & white
    ('Cara', 'Rooster')
Pumpkin
Rocket
Shallots
Spinach, perpetual
Sprouts 'Clodius', 'Bosworth'
Squash
Swede 'Tweed'
Swiss chard
–
Apples (inc. cooking, 'Edward
    VII', 'Lord Derby', 'Howgate
    Wonder')
Pears

BEANS, FRENCH AND RUNNER
Climbing French bean 'Blue Lake', stringless and still
    delicious when the pods are fat
Flat-podded climbing French bean 'Algarve', also stringless
Runner bean 'Aintree', good flavour, stringless,
    self-pollinating
Runner bean 'Enorma', very long, stringless
Runner bean 'Firestorm', good flowers, stringless, red,
    self-pollinating
Runner bean 'Stardust', vigorous, good flavour, stringless,
    self-pollinating
Runner bean 'White Lady', heavy cropper, good setter,
    white flowers

Self-pollinating varieties are the result of crossing a runner
and a French bean: they look like runners and inherit the
characteristic of self-pollinating from the French bean.
Runners are pollinated by bumble bees and need moisture
in the air for a good set, so they really do better in September,
October.

PEAS
SOWN

November	'Douce Provence'	cold frame, planters in March, picking in May
February	'Spring'	very early
March	'Spring'	
	'Hurst Green Shaft'	up to 9 peas per pod
April	'Delikata'	mangetout
	'Sugar Ann'	sugarsnap

POTATOES, 2013
EARLY (JUNE/JULY)
  'Swift'
  'Foremost'
  'Colleen'
SECOND EARLY (AUGUST)
  'Purple Majesty'
SALAD (JULY TO SEPTEMBER)
  'Anya'
  'Bambino'
  'Charlotte'
  'International Kidney'
  'Juliette'
  'Marilyn'
  'Annabelle'
MAINCROP (OCTOBER TO JANUARY, STORED)
  'Sarpo Mira'
  'Cara' (white)
  'Rooster' (red)

TOMATOES
'Andine Cornue'
'Black Cherry'
'Black Krim'
'Bloody Butcher'
'Delicious' (syn. 'Burpee's Delicious')
'Fandango'
'Fantasio'
'Ferline'
'Sweet Million'
'Sweetie'
'Sungold'
'Yellow Pearshaped'

Appendix 4: Flowers grown

BULBS
1 Bulbs for forcing for Christmas
Ordered mid-July, planted mid-September
Hyacinthus orientalis   'Delft Blue'
                     'Pink Pearl'
                     'White Pearl'
Narcissus 'Ziva' (paperwhites, 18-cm/7-inch pots in cold frame, then forced for cutting and use as pot plants)

2 Bulbs mainly for cutting
Also ordered mid-July, planted mid-September
Freesia pale and dark yellow, lavender, red and white, grown in 12-cm/5-inch pots in greenhouse mainly for cutting February to March
Anemones planted outside to flower March to May, not replanted every year
Anemone coronaria (De Caen Group)
    'Hollandia' red
    'Mister Fokker' blue
    'The Bride' white
    'Sylphide' violet rose

3 Bulbs for bedding, naturalizing, cut flowers and pots
Ordered early September, planted end October to November

BEDDING
Hyacinths & tulips

NATURALIZING
Narcissus pseudonarcissus
Narcissus obvallaris
Narcissus poeticus var. *recurvus*
Fritillaria meleagris

CUT FLOWERS AND POTS
Hyacinths for after Christmas (January to April) house decoration
'Aiolos'
'Blue Jacket'
'City of Bradford'
'City of Haarlem'
'Gypsy Queen'
'Jan Bos'
'Minos'
'Miss Saigon'
'Pink Pearl'
'Woodstock'

TULIPS
A selection for cutting from April to end of May, depending on the weather; grown in 30-cm/12-inch pots, 20–25 per pot, taken into greenhouse for forcing

EARLY	'Bellona' yellow
	'Christmas Marvel' (pink, Single Early)
	'Prinses Irene' (orange)
	'Purple Prince' (purple)
MID	'Café Noir' (black)
	'Don Quichotte' (pink)
	'Happy Generation' (red/white)
	'Helmar' (yellow/red (Triumph, like Rembrandt)
	'Negrita' (purple)
	'Peerless Pink' (pink)
	'Rems Favourite' (purple/white,Triumph)
	'White Dream' (white)
FRINGED	'Burgundy Lace' (wine red)
	'Curly Sue' (purple)
	'Fringed Elegance' (pale yellow)
	'Maja' (pale yellow, very late – useful)
	'Red Hat' (red)
DARWIN HYBRID	'Pink Impression'
LILY-FLOWERED	'Ballerina' (orange)
	'Mariette' (pink)
	'Red Shine'
	'West Point' (yellow)
	'White Triumphator'
PARROT	'Apricot Parrot'
	'Blumex' (red/orange)
	'Estella Rijnveld' (white/red)
	'Orange Favourite'
	(Some Parrot varieties have weak stems.)
SINGLE LATE	'Avignon' (red)
	'Dordogne' (tangerine)
	'Maureen' (ivory)
	'Menton' (peachy pink)
	'Queen of Night' (black, most useful, keeping flowers going until end of May
	'Sorbet' (pink/white, classic tulip shape)

SWEET PEAS AND OTHER *LATHYRUS*
Varieties for October sowing
'Angela Ann'
'Anniversary'
'Bouquet Crimson'
'Bouquet White'
'Cathy'
'Charlie's Angels'
'Dark Passion'
'Eclipse'
'Ethel Grace'
'Evening Glow'
'Lizbeth'
'Milly'
'Noel Sutton'
'Richard and Judy'
'Valerie Harrod'
'White Frills'

Varieties for January–March sowing
'Dorothy Eckford'
'Heathcliff'
'King Edward'
'Matucana'
'Miss Willmott'
'Prince Edward of York'

Also chosen, some species *Lathyrus*
Lathyrus nervosus
Lathyrus pubescens
Lathyrus sativus
Lathyrus sativus f. *albus*

CHRYSANTHEMUMS
Lifted, potted and overwintered under cold glass. In January, brought into 5°C/41°F to produce cuttings for next season's plants.
'Bretforton Road'
'Capel Manor'
'Cousin Joan'
'Emperor of China'
'Hazel'
'Ruby Mound'
'Uri'
'Wedding Day'
'Winning's Red'

DAHLIAS
For cutting August, September, October

RED	'Bishop of Llandaff'
	'John Street'
DEEP RED	'Aurora's Kiss'
	'Chat Noir'
	'Jescot Nubia'
	'Jowey Mirella'
	'Rip City'
	'Sam Hopkins'
ORANGE	'David Howard'
	'Ludwig Helfert'
YELLOW	'Glorie van Heemstede'
	'Jescot Buttercup'
LILAC	'Bonny Blue'
	'Worton Blue Streak'
PURPLE	'Hillcrest Royale'
	'Winston Churchill'
WHITE	'Karma Serena'
	unidentified white Cactus from Rousham
	'Vivian Russell'
PINK	'Gerrie Hoek'
	'Pearl of Heemstede'
	'Piper's Pink'

DIANTHUS
Pinks
'Cranberry Ice'
'Devon Siskin' (Raspberry Swirl)
'Gran's Favourite'
'Laced Joy'
'London Lovely'
'Red Welsh'
'Rose de Mai'
'Strawberry Sorbet'
'Valda Wyatt'

Malmaison carnations
'Duchess of Westminster'
'Princess of Wales'
'Souvenir de la Malmaison' (syn. 'Old Blush')
'Tayside Red'
'Thora'

GALANTHUS
Galanthus 'Atkinsii'
Galanthus elwesii
Galanthus elwesii 'Godfrey Owen'
Galanthus elwesii 'Mrs Macnamara'
Galanthus elwesii 'Peter Gatehouse'
Galanthus elwesii 'Selborne Green Tips'
Galanthus 'Emerald'
Galanthus 'Faringdon Double'
Galanthus 'Galatea'
Galanthus 'Hill Poë'
Galanthus 'Hippolyta'
Galanthus 'Jacquenetta'
Galanthus 'John Gray'
Galanthus 'Limetree'
Galanthus 'Magnet'
Galanthus 'Merlin'
Galanthus nivalis
Galanthus nivalis 'Bitton'
Galanthus nivalis f. *pleniflorus* 'Blewbury Tart'
Galanthus nivalis f. *pleniflorus* 'Lady Elphinstone'
Galanthus 'Ophelia'
Galanthus plicatus (Crimean snowdrop)

Galanthus plicatus 'Augustus'
Galanthus plicatus 'Colossus'
Galanthus plicatus 'Diggory'
Galanthus plicatus 'Warham'
Galanthus 'Robin Hood'
Galanthus 'S. Arnott'

HEDYCHIUMS
Stock of each of these kept in the glasshouses, under the staging, while still dormant
Hedychium coronarium
Hedychium densiflorum 'Assam Orange'
Hedychium densiflorum 'Sorung'
Hedychium densiflorum 'Stephen'
Hedychium gardnerianum
Hedychium greenii

HELIOTROPES (*Heliotropium arborescens*)
Overwintered in the glasshouses
'Chatsworth'
'Dame Alice de Hales'
'Gatton Park'
'Lord Roberts'
'Mrs J.W. Lowther'
'Princess Marina'
'The Speaker'
'W.H. Lowther'
'White Lady'
'White Princess'

NERINES
Grown under glass
Nerine sarniensis
Nerine sarniensis var. *corusca* (syn. *N. corusca* 'Major')
Nerine undulata
Nerine sarniensis hybrids:
'Afterglow'
'Baghdad'
'Belladonna'
'Bennett-Poë'
'Grania'
'Hanley Castle'
'Jenny Wren'
'Lady Cynthia Colville'
'Lady Eleanor Keane'
'Mother of Pearl'
'Ophelia'
'Pink Galore'
'Pink Triumph'
'Rose Princess'
'Rushmere Star'
'Salmon Supreme'
'Terry Jones'
'Virgo'
'Wolsey'

Hardier sorts grown out of doors for cutting
Nerine bowdenii
Nerine bowdenii 'Marjorie'
Nerine bowdenii 'Mollie Cowie'
Nerine bowdenii 'Ostara'
Nerine bowdenii 'Patricia'
Nerine bowdenii 'Quinton Wells'
Nerine bowdenii 'Ruth'
Nerine bowdenii 'Sheila Owen'

PELARGONIUMS

Planted out in beds or pots or displayed in number 2 greenhouse in summer, moved to number 5 greenhouse in winter for propagation and growing on

CLASSIFICATION

d	double (in combination)
Dec	Decorative
I	Ivy-leaved
R	Regal
Sc	Scented-leaved
St	Stellar (in combination)
U	Unique
v	variegated (in combination)
Z	Zonal

'Apple Blossom Rosebud'	Z/d
'Arctic Star'	Z/St
'Ardens'	
'Atomic Snowflake'	Sc/v
australe	
'Carisbrooke'	R
'Charity'	Sc
'Chocolate Peppermint' (entrance bedding)	Sc
'Clorinda'	U/Sc
'Copthorne'	U/Sc
cordifolium	Sc
'Cousin Dolly'	Z
'Crimson Unique'	U
crispum 'Variegatum'	Sc/v
'Crystal Palace Gem'	Z/v
denticulatum	Sc
denticulatum 'Filicifolium' (auricula theatre)	Sc
'Duchess of Devonshire'	U
'Fair Ellen'	Sc
Fireworks White ('Fiwowit')	Z/St
'Frank Headley'	Z/v
'Gartendirektor Herman'	Dec
'Grey Lady Plymouth'	Sc/v
'Hederinum Variegatum' (syn. 'Duke of Edinburgh')	I/v
'Hermione'	Z/d
'Hindoo'	R×U
'Hula'	R×U
'Lady Ilchester'	Z/d
'Lady Plymouth'	Sc/v
'L'Elégante'	I/v
'Lord Bute'	R
'Madame Auguste Nonin' (syn. 'Monsieur Ninon')	U/Sc
'Moreanum' (syns 'Moore's Victory', 'More's Victory, 'Scarlet Pet')	U
'Mr Wren'	Z
'Paton's Unique'	U/Sc
'Paul Crampel'	Z
'Peppermint Lace'	Sc
'Prince of Orange'	Sc
'Radula'	Sc
'Red Rambler'	Z/d
'Rober's Lemon Rose'	Sc
'Royal Ascot'	R
'Royal Black Rose'	I/d
'Shottesham Pet' (syn. 'Concolor Lace')	Sc
Solo ('Giullio']	Z×I
'Sweet Mimosa'	Sc
tomentosum	Sc
'Vera Dillon'	Z
'Voodoo'	R×U
'Welling'	Sc
'Wilhelm Langguth' ('Caroline Schmidt' misapplied)	Z/d/v
'Yale'	I/d

OLD ROSES IN THE ROSE BORDERS
Favourites marked with asterisks
Dates added where known

'Adam Messerich' Bourbon 1920
'Baronne Prévost' Hybrid Perpetual * 1842
'Boule de Neige' Bourbon 1867
'Commandant Beaurepaire' Bourbon 1874
'Coupe d'Hébé' Bourbon 1840
'De Resht' Portland c.1840
'Duke of Edinburgh' Hybrid Perpetual 1868
'Ferdinand Pichard' Hybrid Perpetual 1921
'Gros Chou de Hollande' Bourbon*
'Honorine de Brabant' striped Bourbon
'Louise Odier' Bourbon*1851
'Mme Boll' (syn. 'Comte de Chambord') Portland* 1859
'Mme Ernest Calvat' Bourbon 1888
'Mme Isaac Pereire' Bourbon 1881
'Mme Pierre Oger' Bourbon 1878
'Paul Verdier' Bourbon 1866
'Reine des Violettes' Hybrid Perpetual* 1860
'Reine Victoria' Bourbon 1872
'Souvenir du Docteur Jamain' Hybrid Perpetual 1865
'Variegata di Bologna' Bourbon 1909

SALVIA COLLECTION
Stock of the following overwintered in the glasshouses

Salvia 'African Sky'
Salvia 'Amistad'
Salvia atrocyanea
Salvia 'Black Knight'
Salvia blepharophylla
Salvia blepharophylla 'Diablo'
Salvia buchananii
Salvia 'Christine Yeo'
Salvia clevelandii
Salvia clevelandii 'Winnifred Gilman'
Salvia concolor
Salvia confertiflora
Salvia curviflora
Salvia darcyi
Salvia discolor
Salvia dombeyi
Salvia elegans 'Scarlet Pineapple'
Salvia elegans 'Tangerine'
Salvia fulgens
Salvia greggii 'Alba'
Salvia greggii 'Lara'
Salvia greggii 'Lipstick'
Salvia greggii 'Peach'
Salvia greggii 'Pink Preference'
Salvia greggii 'Stormy Pink'
Salvia greggii × serpyllifolia (Salvia coahuilensis misapplied)
Salvia guaranitica 'Argentina Skies'
Salvia guaranitica 'Black and Blue'
Salvia guaranitica 'Blue Enigma'
Salvia haenkei 'Prawn Chorus'
Salvia 'Indigo Spires'
Salvia involucrata
Salvia involucrata 'Bethellii'
Salvia involucrata 'Boutin'
Salvia involucrata 'Joan'
Salvia × jamensis 'Hot Lips'
Salvia × jamensis 'La Luna'
Salvia × jamensis 'Nachtvlinder'
Salvia × jamensis 'Peter Vidgeon'
Salvia × jamensis 'Raspberry Royale'
Salvia × jamensis 'Red Velvet'
Salvia × jamensis 'Señorita Leah'
Salvia × jamensis 'Sierra San Antonio'
Salvia × jamensis 'Trebah'
Salvia lanceolata
Salvia 'Lemon Pie'

Salvia leucantha
Salvia leucantha 'Purple Velvet'
Salvia leucantha 'Santa Barbara'
Salvia macrophylla
Salvia maderensis
Salvia microphylla 'Belize'
Salvia microphylla 'Lutea'
Salvia microphylla 'Wild Watermelon'
Salvia 'Mulberry Jam'
Salvia Mystic Spires Blue ('Balsalmisp')
Salvia oxyphora
Salvia 'Pam's Purple'
Salvia patens, Derry Watkins' giant form
Salvia patens 'White Trophy'
Salvia 'Penny's Smile'
Salvia 'Phyllis' Fancy'
Salvia 'Purple Majesty'
Salvia regla
Salvia repens
Salvia 'Royal Bumble'
Salvia 'Silas Dyson'
Salvia 'Silke's Dream'
Salvia splendens 'Jimi's Good Red'
Salvia splendens 'Van-Houttei'
Salvia stolonifera
Salvia 'Trelissick'
Salvia 'Trelawney'
Salvia uliginosa
Salvia uliginosa 'Ballon Azul'
Salvia 'Waverly'
Salvia 'Wendy's Wish'

POT PLANTS
For use under glass and indoors
Adiantum venustum (maidenhair fern)
Aspidistra elatior 'Variegata'
Begonia 'Escargot'
Cyclamen persicum (various cultivars for house decoration, including large-flowered in red, white and pink plus small-flowered, scented white – different cultivars chosen from year to year)
Davallia canariensis (hare's foot fern)
Dypsis lutescens (syn. *Chrysalidocarpus l.*) palm
Cypripedium orchid
Coelogyne orchid
Hedera helix
Nephrolepis
Plectranthus
Pteris cretica (Cretan brake fern)
Pteris cretica var. *albolineata* (white striped)
Pteris cretica 'Alexandrae' (cristate)
Sinningia tubiflora
Streptocarpus 'Albatross'
Streptocarpus 'Constant Nymph'
Streptocarpus saxorum

TENDER PLANTS FOR OUTDOOR USE IN SUMMER
In glasshouses during winter, to maintain stock
and for propagation
Abutilon 'Boule de Neige'
Abutilon 'Canary Bird'
Abutilon 'Nabob'
Abutilon 'Waltz'
Aeonium arboreum
Aeonium 'Blushing Beauty'
Aeonium 'Zwartkop'
Agave americana 'Mediopicta Alba'
Aloysia citrodora (syn. *Lippia citriodora*)
Anisodontea 'El Rayo'
Arctotis 'Red Magic'
Argyranthemum gracile 'Chelsea Girl'
Argyranthemum 'Jamaica Primrose'

Argyranthemum 'Vancouver'
Astelia
Azorina vidalii
Azorina vidalii 'Rosea'
Begonia grandis subsp. *evansiana*
Beschorneria yuccoides
Bidens aurea
Brugmansia yellow
Canna × *ehemanii* (*C. iridiflora* misapplied)
Canna 'Richard Wallace'
Cordyline australis
Cosmos atrosanguineus
Diascia integerrima
Diascia personata
Diascia Redstart ('Hecstart')
Diascia rigescens
Diascia 'White Icicle'
Dierama pulcherrimum
Fascicularia bicolor
Francoa ramosa
Felicia amelloides 'Santa Anita'
Helichrysum petiolare 'Limelight'
Impatiens ugandensis
Jasminum polyanthum
Laurus nobilis bay laurel
Lavandula × *christiana*
Lavandula dentata
Lotus berthelotii
Lotus jacobaeus
Mimulus aurantiacus
Mimulus 'Popacatapetl'
Nierembergia scoparia (syn. *N. frutescens*)
Osteospermum 'Buttermilk'
Osteospermum 'Sparkler'
Osteospermum 'Whirlygig'
Osteospermum 'White Pim' (syn. *O. ecklonis* var. *prostratum*)
Penstemon 'Alice Hindley'
Penstemon 'Andenken an Friedrich Hahn' (syn. *P.* 'Garnet')
Penstemon 'Blackbird'
Penstemon 'Evelyn'
Penstemon 'Jill Lucas'
Penstemon 'King George V'
Plumbago auriculata dark blue
Plumbago auriculata pale blue
Plumbago auriculata f. *alba* white
pomegranate
Puya alpestris
Scabiosa atropurpurea 'Ace of Spades'
Sollya heterophylla blue
Sollya heterophylla 'Alba'
Verbena bonariensis
Verbena 'Diamond Purple'
Verbena 'Diamond Merci'
Verbena 'Diamond Topaz'
Verbena peruviana
Verbena rigida f. *lilacina* 'Polaris'
Verbena Seabrook's Lavender ('Sealav')
Verbena 'Sissinghurst'
Zantedeschia, pink throat

Appendix 5: Annual seed sowing

This is a carefully organized operation under glass (in the propagation greenhouse) so that there is a constant production line, with enough space allowed to keep the succession going before things can be hardened off outside.

Week 2   (January) *Persicaria orientalis* (syn. *Polygonum orientale*), *Francoa ramosa* cold house
Week 6   Sweet peas, *Cobaea*, basil, alpine strawberry, *Salvia patens*, *Nepeta govaniana*, parsley, *Antirrhinum*, *Lobelia cardinalis*
Week 8   Celery, celeriac, aubergine
Week 9   (March) *Nicotiana mutabilis*, *Dactylicapnos scandens* (syn. *Dicentra scandens*), thyme, basil, *Phlox*, *Rudbeckia*, cornflower
Week 11   *Callistephus chinensis* (syn. *Aster chinensis*), *Cordyline*, *Cleome*, winter savory, *Omphalodes linifolia*, scabious
Week 12   Tomatoes, peppers, melons, basil, *Tagetes*, borage

Week 13   *Verbascum*
Week 14   *Ammi majus*, *Orlaya grandiflora*, *Viola*, basil, *Cerinthe*, *Malope*, *Nigella*, *Agrostis*, *Tithonia*
Week 15   Cucumber, *Cosmos*, cornflower, pot marigold
Week 16   *Nicotiana suaveolens*, basil
Week 17   Scabious, *Salvia* (biennials)
Week 18   (May) *Zinnia*, nasturtium, *Tagetes*
Week 20   Sweet williams, sunflowers
Week 22   Foxgloves
Week 24   Polyanthus, *Myosotis*
Week 27   (June) *Aquilegia*, wallflowers
Week 28   Iceland poppies
Week 40   Sweet peas

Appendix 6: Seed collection

Seeds of the following collected in 2012

Alcea rosea
Alonsoa meridionalis
Alstroemeria ligtu hybrids
Aquilegia long-spurred yellow
Azorina vidalii 'Rosea'
Borago officinalis 'Alba'
Borago pygmaea
Browallia americana 'Alba'
Canna indica
Cerinthe major 'Purpurascens'
Cleome hassleriana deep pink
Cobaea scandens f. *alba*
Dactylicapnos scandens (syn. *Dicentra scandens*)
Dahlia coccinea wine
Delphinium mixed
Delphinium staphisagria
Digitalis purpurea f. *albiflora*
Eccremocarpus scaber red
Eccremocarpus scaber 'Tresco Cream'
Eryngium giganteum
Francoa ramosa
Lathyrus latifolius 'White Pearl'
Lathyrus rotundifolius
Leonotis nepetifolia from South America

Linaria purpurea 'Brown's White'
Lychnis coronaria
Malope trifida 'Alba' from South America
Nepeta govaniana
Nicotiana longiflora from South America
Nicotiana mutabilis
Nicotiana suaveolens
Nicotiana sylvestris
Nicotiana ex Rousham green
Nigella damascena 'Miss Jekyll Alba'
Nigella damascena 'Miss Jekyll'
Oenothera odorata cream-flowered
Omphalodes linifolia
Persicaria orientalis
Psylliostachys suworowii from South America
Salvia patens
Salvia patens 'Cambridge Blue'
Salvia sclarea var. *turkestanica*
Scabiosa atropurpurea 'Ace of Spades'
Scabiosa caucasica 'Kompliment'
Silene coeli-rosa 'Blue Angel' from South America
Silybum marianum
Tagetes from Himalayas
Zantedeschia pink throat from South Africa

BIBLIOGRAPHY

Blacker, Mary Rose, *Flora Domestica: A History of British Flower Arranging 1500–1930*, Abrams, New York, 2000
Coats, Alice M., *Flowers and their Histories*, A&C Black, London, 1968
Elliott, Brent, *Victorian Gardens*, Batsford, London, 1986
Morgan, Joan and Alison Richards, *A Paradise out of a Common Field: The Pleasures and Plenty of the Victorian Garden*, Century, London, 1990

Quest-Ritson, Charles, *The English Garden Abroad*, Viking, New York and London, 1986
Rothschild, Mrs James A. de, *The Rothschilds at Waddesdon Manor*, Collins, London, 1979
From the Waddesdon archive
   Gaucher, Marcel, diary entry on gardening
   Knox, Tim, Report on Eythrope, 2002
   Rothschild, Miss Alice, letters to her head gardener, G.F. Johnson

Page numbers in *italics* refer to illustrations.

ACKNOWLEDGMENTS

My thanks to the Rothschild family for proposing and backing this book and to Sue Dickinson, Jonathan Cooke, Tim Hicks and the Eythrope team for endless answers to my questions. The archivists at Waddesdon and Fiona Sinclair provided unfailing support. Jo Christian and Pimpernel Press saw the book through to its accelerated deadlines. Tony Lord prevented botanical howlers, Tom Hatton and Dean Pauley, the hard-working photographer and graphic designer, came down to see me for many working sessions on layout. Pip Morrison, Jane Barnwell and Philippa Lewis made helpful comments. Faber and Faber kindly waived the copyright fee for Alice Oswald's poems. Thanks to all of them and especially to Charles Keen, to whom I promised, twenty years ago, that I would never write another book.

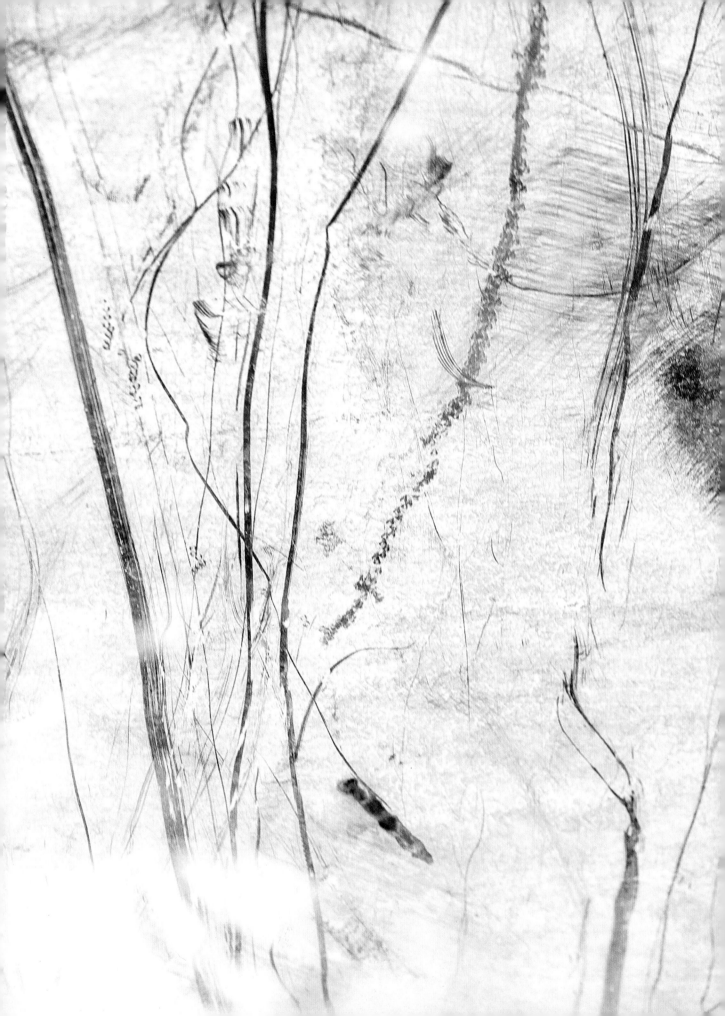